Restaurant Biz
is
SHOWBIZ!

ABOUT THE COVER

Teamwork is important to the success of any business, but especially to the restaurant business and to show business, the intertwined themes of this book.

The most exciting example of teamwork in show business is the high-kicking chorus line epitomized by the Radio City Music Hall Rockettes. Our cover shows what a high-kicking restaurant chorus line might look like. Note, however, that one of the team has the wrong leg in the air.

This is to underline how important it is to engage an accountant who understands the complexity of the restaurant business, the critical role of marketing to a restaurant's success and why "accepted accounting cost formulas" are not always acceptable.

For many of you, your restaurant will be a big part of your life. Take the time to select an accountant who is knowledgable about and cares about the restaurant business, and who concurs with your vision of what you want your restaurant to be. Then heed the advice you get.

Cover illustration and layout; illustration on back page: Frank Springer

ABOUT THE EDITOR

Editors take the raw material produced by writers, or in my case, reporters, digest what is being said, and then ask questions that require us to dig deeper into each interview and into each set of opinions to capture as much meat as we can. Then, editors apply their skills to polish the new words of wisdom into even more pleasing form.

Dinah Witchel edited this book and I believe she has done a remarkable job. A journalist and author in her own right, she knows what it is like to be blue-pencilled. So when she is wearing her editor's hat, she emphasizes using her blue pencil to enhance the writer's voice. That is, my words sound like me, but better.

Restaurant Biz
is
SHOWBIZ!

Why Marketing is the Key to Your Success

by

Dave Steadman

Whittier Green Publishing Co. Inc.

Restaurant Biz is Show Biz!
Copyright © 1991 David Steadman.

Although the author and publisher have made extensive efforts to
ensure the accuracy and completeness of the information contained
in this book, we assume no responsibility for errors, inaccuracies,
omissions or inconsistencies herein. The honest opinions of one
person might contradict the honest opinions of the next. Readers will
have to weigh one set of comments against others appearing in this
book and conclude for themselves what is useful. Any slights against
people or organizations are unintentional.
In no case should readers rely exclusively on material in this book to
plan or operate a restaurant. Attorneys, accountants and other experts
with restaurant experience should be consulted.

Published by
Whittier Green Publishing Co. Inc.,
67 Broadway,
Greenlawn, N.Y. 11740.

Typeset by
Maxim's Page Design Inc.
448 Lenox Road
Huntington Station, N.Y. 11746

Printed and bound in the United States of America by Arcata
Graphics Fairfield, Fairfield, Pennsylvania. All rights reserved.
No part of this book may be reproduced in any form or by any
electronic or mechanical means including information storage and
retrieval systems without permission in writing from the publisher,
except by a reviewer, who may quote brief passages in a review.

Library of Congress Catalog Card Number: 91-65277
ISBN 0-9628954-0-7

**Dedicated to
Kathleen Geyer Steadman**

ACKNOWLEDGMENTS

Thank you to all of the people you will meet in the following chapters who willingly shared their knowledge of the restaurant business for the benefit of you, who one day may be their competitors.

And appreciation to my family, friends and acquaintances who made important contributions to the completion of this book, often without knowing it. My children, Cecelia, Mary and David, and Roy Anderson, Dennis Beacham, Bill Bennett, Jeff Berlind, Bill Bertholf, Charles Broffman, Joe Ciardullo, John Delves, Henry Ehle, Bob Farrell, Bill Fermoile, Jean Fermoile, Alice Fuller, Walter Hasson, Dick Howard, S.M. Kathleen Thomas, Brendan Kelly, Joe Kelly, Don Komisarow, Herman Levy, John Malloy, George McCarthy, Bob Melton, Mac Moore, Chuck Murray, Brian 'Bud' Palmer, Wally Patterson, Bob Poulin, Don Rayle, Dick Reumann, John Shields, Marty Steadman, Peggy Steadman, Rick Wyckoff, and Catharina Young.

RESTAURANT BIZ Is SHOW BIZ!
Why Marketing is the Key to Your Success
By DAVE STEADMAN

TABLE OF CONTENTS

PART III: EXPERT ADVICE

PART IV: SIGNATURE RECIPES

INDEX TO RESTAURANTS

INDEX TO PEOPLE

RESTAURANT TRADE MAGAZINES

INTRODUCTION

So you want to open your own restaurant. Or perhaps own part of a restaurant. You'll be a working partner. Or a passive investor.

It doesn't bother you that over 75 percent of all new restaurants are not going to make it. Your place is going to be a winner.

The good news is that your restaurant can beat the odds. The not-so-good news is that you are going to be working longer and harder than you ever expected.

Even as a passive investor you will be spending a lot of time at "your" restaurant. Hell, that's most of the fun. At least it's fun while things are going well. If business is not good, you'll be frustrated at not being able to pinpoint a problem and make intelligent and workable suggestions to your partner(s).

Your options: A) close your eyes, enjoy being an owner as long as the restaurant stays open and figure it's more fun losing money this way than at the race track, or B) start learning about the restaurant business so that you can pitch in to protect your investment and point with pride when you introduce friends and business associates to *your* restaurant.

Keep reading if you chose "B."

Here's your eight-point program for a successful restaurant.

1) Good location.
2) Proper equipment and supplies.
3) Professional kitchen staff.
4) Adequate initial financing.
5) Honest bartenders.
6) Experienced management and floor staff.
7) No compromises on the quality of the food.
8) Only quality products at the bar.

1

With all of this, the odds are still against success. You also have to understand marketing and merchandising.

People don't go to restaurants just to be fed. They can order a pizza or dim sum if they don't want to cook. Customers at fine restaurants want to be made to feel special.

Going to a restaurant is a social experience, an opportunity to meet old friends, make new friends, be dazzled by exciting food presentations, tempted by new drink concoctions or a bartender who knows how to make the perfect Martini, entertained after dinner at a piano bar or with a jazz combo.

But with or without entertainment, when you're in the restaurant business you're in Show Business. That's what this book is all about.

In the first eight chapters are my thoughts about how you can establish a solid foundation on which to build. The next sections feature secrets of successful restaurateurs and advice from respected industry consultants and other industry specialists on how they can work with you in your quest for success.

The opinions in the first eight chapters come from my 25 years of professional involvement with restaurateurs, beginning with the years I spent with *Restaurant Hospitality* magazine from 1965 through 1970, and including stints as editor and publisher of *Ideas for Restaurant Profits* and *Beverage Profit Ideas*, a magazine for beverage managers and bartenders.

In that time I have eaten in more than 2,500 restaurants and spoken at length with restaurant owners and their staffs. I took particular note of what the successful restaurateurs were doing that the less successful were not.

There are many ideas in this book that will save you heartache and make you money. Let's start with the best idea first.

Part I

WORDS OF WISDOM

1

QUALITY

We are a brand-name society. We associate well-known brands with quality. Supermarkets stock house brands and no-name generics, but in the shopping baskets at the checkout counters are the names synonymous with quality: Coca-Cola, Pepsi Cola, Campbell's, Heinz, Perdue, and so on.

It's the same in a package store. There are many inexpensive brands of alcoholic beverages, but the best selling products are the well-known brands: Bacardi rum, Smirnoff vodka, Seagram's whiskey. With Scotch, gin, wine, beer, it is recognizable names of quality that are most in demand.

Your customers, too, want quality, expect quality, and are willing to pay for quality. But do they know from the moment they walk into your restaurant that you stand for quality?

Many customers will be introduced to your restaurant at your bar, waiting to be seated for a meal or meeting a friend. What do these brand-conscious customers see as they sit? The first impression is often of a bartender pouring no-name brands. Sometimes they'll hear a waitress specify a name

"In this business, change is constant. But certain things never change. You always have to be proud of what you serve and how you serve it."

PHIL LEHR
Phil Lehr's Steakery
San Francisco,
California

4

brand and watch the bartender pour Brand X because he doesn't think the customer can tell the difference.

That's sending mixed signals.

The menu brags about the quality of the food, the drink list spotlights elegant house specialty drinks, and the wine list bespeaks a connoisseur. What's more, the prices probably reflect the quality so highly touted.

But when the bartender pours brands that few customers would offer to guests in their homes, don't you think there will be some wondering about the quality of the foods coming from the kitchen, conveniently out of sight?

Of course, you only use high quality food in your kitchen and you brag in your advertising and on the menu about your high standards. Do the same at your bar.

Stock only quality brands and tell your customers with pride what brands you pour when they don't specify a choice. Seeing name brands poured at the bar, customers will readily believe your claims about food standards.

Just as customers seated at table will eventually read everything on the table including the backs of sugar packets, customers at the bar "read" the back bar.

What do they generally see?

A work station for the bartender with glassware, bar checks, and brands lined up according to frequency of call. This is valuable selling space being wasted.

> *"Restaurant owners have to talk to their customers on a regular basis. If the customer is not happy with the food he is served, it doesn't matter how good the owner, chef, or manager thinks it is. The only one that really counts is the customer."*
> **MICHAEL HERNANDEZ**
> Michael's Cafe, Bar & Grill
> Naples, Florida

Your Back Bar Is Macy's Window

Think of the back bar as Macy's window. Here is where your customers discover that you care enough about them to pour only quality brands. Here is their cue that your restaurant is the place to visit to take their

5

first taste of that new liqueur or cognac or single malt Scotch that they have heard about.

On a shelf labeled "Our House Brands," place your pouring brands. When you decide to change any pouring brand, just replace the appropriate bottle—but be certain that customers perceive the change as an improvement.

New products are continually being introduced in the spirits world. Ask your salesmen for advance notice of items that will receive heavy introductory promotion in your area.

Call attention to these products on your back bar. Put one on a pedestal, shine a spotlight on it, and offer it at an alluring introductory price. Create a special drink.

During weeks when nothing is new, dust off a bottle that hasn't had much call, create a new drink or resurrect an oldy but goody. Give it the star treatment for a week, again at a reduced price.

You may take some kidding at first, but in time customers will count on trying a new beverage at your place. They'll look for it on the back bar and ask what drink you've created now.

Analyze what your customers ask for. If many regulars order Scotch, set apart an area of the back bar to display a variety of super-premium Scotch whiskys, including at least six brands of single malt Scotch. To start, order mixed cases of two or three bottles of each brand.

Display special tasting glasses and suggest a comparison tasting, selecting three brands and pouring 1/2 ounce of each, combined with 1/2 ounce of water. Provide crackers and a glass of water to clear the palate between tastes. Invite an open discussion of the differing flavors and record comments in

"Good food, good drink, and good customers make for success. The most important is good customers, because they attract more of the same kind. "
GARLAND FLAHERTY
Flaherty's III
Louisville, Kentucky

a book kept at the bar where customers may consult it freely.

This merchandising technique can work equally as well for premium vodkas, brandies, or liqueurs.

For the bar customers who want a non-alcoholic beverage, your back bar can also showcase a selection of non-alcoholic beers, wines, champagnes, sparkling ciders, and waters of the world.

There are excellent products now available in all of these categories, as well as non-alcoholic *creme de menthe, creme de cacao,* and other liqueurs, allowing you to broaden your "virgin drinks" to include grasshoppers, *creme frappes,* and other traditional cocktails.

It all spells quality! Don't devalue your whole restaurant by pinching pennies at the bar. Quality has to be at the heart of your operation.

> *"We do pea soup well and we make the most out of that."*
> **REY BENITEZ**
> Pea Soup
> Andersen's
> Buellton, California

2

STRESS VALUE

Serve the finest quality food and beverages, price them reasonably, and you can still acquire a reputation as an "expensive" restaurant, a special occasion destination.

The seats will be filled on weekends and holidays, but there are 250 other under-occupied days and nights.

What can you do?

A) Keep your costs the same but reduce prices. Gross profit will be less, but maybe you'll make it up in volume.

B) Keep gross profits steady by reducing menu prices and food costs. Translation: lower quality.

C) Develop "perceived value." Communicate with your customers so that they appreciate the value you're giving them.

A and B are dead ends. C is the answer.

But how do you heighten perceived value?

First, let's look at some common examples of customer turn-offs:

1) They arrive on time for their reservation, are told there will be a "short wait," and are steered to the bar.

2) The person who's a sport on an expense account would like to come back on

> "Restaurant guests want value, good service, interesting food, and a comfortable decor. I believe we'll continue to prosper as long as we remember this and never take our business for granted."
>
> **LYDIA SHIRE**
> Biba Restaurant
> Boston,
> Massachusetts

his own, but is more value conscious when it's his own money he's spending.

3) Most customers will not complain about sub-par food, even when asked "How is everything?" Dissatisfied customers just don't come back and they also warn their friends and acquaintances away. You probably won't even know why.

4) Some people on diets are careful of what they order, but most people don't want to be reminded of calorie counts.They are charmed when assured (tongue in cheek) that the triple chocolate layer cake has had all of the calories removed.

5) People think that restaurants charge outrageous prices for wine, and 90 percent of the time they are right.

6) Cognac drinkers will never believe that one-and-a-half ounces of cognac served in a large snifter is worth the price that restaurants charge for cognac.

7) Smokers resent being treated like second-class citizens.

> "The public wants value. The big growth is in the middle, restaurants offering very good food at reasonable prices. The culinary schools are providing people capable of becoming good creative chefs, so the talent is there."
>
> **TONY MAY**
> San Domenico NY,
> La Camelia,
> Sandro's
> New York, New York

Negatives Become Positives

Now let's turn these legitimate concerns into perceived value.

1) When tables aren't turning quickly and you can't seat people promptly, give something to those with reservations who arrived on time. Offer a drink at the bar while they wait or a free dessert or liqueur after dinner.

2) Your expense account customer returns on his own because he enjoys the ambience as well as the food. But spending his own money, he can't afford the offerings on your menu that he usually orders. Give this customer a place to go on the menu.

If you're famous for your prime, aged steaks, brag also about your "signature" hip steak (a less expensive cut that can be offered at a much lower price) and the great chopped sirloin smothered with onions. Team sliced sirloin steak with an "extraordinary" steak sauce and world famous home fries, again priced considerably under the prime steaks.

Apply this principle to any type of menu, taking higher mark-up percentages on the less expensive offerings, but still offering recognizable value.

3) Train your waiters, waitresses, and captains to be specific. Asking "How's your food?" ranks right up there with the classic "We must get together sometime." Immediately after food is served ask, "Is the soup hot enough? Is your steak rare, as you requested? Is your lobster tender? Is your fish as firm as you like it?"

If there is hesitation in the customer's response, pursue it immediately. The waiter should be authorized to correct the problem, even if it means replacing the food. If you have a chef who takes returned food as a personal affront, re-educate the chef. If that doesn't work, replace the chef.

Always be gracious. If you're going to replace something, a surly attitude will undo all the good will you should be garnering from accommodating a dissatisfied patron.

Even when a customer is being unreasonable, you win nothing by insisting that the customer is wrong and you are right. Much better to let others in the dining room see you as gracious and quick to please, even if you privately tell the troublesome customer not to come back.

4) Many of your customers will be celebrating. It won't always be a birthday, anniversary, or holiday but frequently something as simple as making a big sale, finishing spring cleaning, or being with a new friend.

> *"I believe an important part of our success has been that there has always been one of the principals here to talk to customers and make them feel as comfortable as if they were home in their own living rooms."*
>
> **BILLY ADER**
> The 1800 Club
> Miami, Florida

Celebrating means finishing a meal with a flourish: A really special dessert or an Irish coffee or a cognac. Perhaps capuccino laced with brandy or espresso with a glass of Sambucca.

But most of the time they'll just ask for coffee and the check.

Why?

Nobody presented an alternative. "Coffee? Does anybody want dessert? How about apple pie?" just doesn't cut it. There's no excitement. Nothing to overcome the automatic "No, thank you," a conditioned response brought on by too many desserts in the past that weren't worth the money or the calories.

Make your desserts truly outstanding. When dinner dishes have been cleared, bring your dessert selection to the table and rhapsodize over each one.

If one person orders a dessert, the rest of the party will often follow suit. Desserts or liqueurs boost the check, generate a bigger tip, and customers have a memorable finish to their meal.

A win-win happening.

> *"Enthusiasm is contagious. If I'm having fun, my employees and customers get caught up in it and everyone is soon having fun. And that's what keeps customers coming back."*
> **DANTE STEPHENSEN**
> Dante's Down the Hatch
> Atlanta, Georgia

About Expensive Wine

5) Understand something. Many people drink good wine with their food at home. Walk into the retail wine stores near you and watch what's happening. People browse, ask questions, buy a number of different labels, sometimes buy cases at a time.

Open your newspaper on the day of the week that wine retailers advertise. A full page ad in *The New York Times* isn't cheap. When the same wine merchants repeatedly pay for retail ads in a major metropolitan daily, it's because that works. People are reading the ads and spending money on wine.

11

Visit the periodical section of your public library and discover how many magazines are writing about wine and how many publications are devoted almost exclusively to wine.

What happens when this well-read public walks into a restaurant with an overpriced wine list. They're insulted, that's what happens. And they refuse to be bullied into paying exorbitant prices for what they know to be inferior wines.

You can walk into dozens of wine stores even in Manhattan, and purchase estate-bottled Bordeaux wine for anywhere from $5 to $15 and get some very good wines.

Try to spot an estate-bottled Bordeaux on a restaurant wine list for less than $20. The same holds true for other very good wines from around the world, California, and other U. S. wine regions.

Cater to America's wine lovers. Offer good wines that you've bought at good value, marked up reasonably. Your customers will not only return, they'll tell their friends about your restaurant.

To build a sensible and adequate wine list, start by talking to salesmen. You'll have to work with at least three different suppliers, perhaps as many as seven or more. Nobody has a corner on good wines and if you don't maintain wide contacts, you will miss out on opportune buys.

Attend wine tastings whenever possible and don't be afraid to ask questions, even if they seem dumb.

Visit nearby wine stores and discover which are most knowledgable and most successful in selling wine. Introduce yourself to the buyers for these stores. They can tell you what wines are popular, what are good values, and which suppliers and salespeople are informed and cooperative.

"Don't worry about other restaurants, pay attention to your own operation. There's always a reason for slow business and it almost always can be traced to how well you and your people are serving your customers."
DAVID GHATANFARD
Edmondo's, Ciao's East Chester, New York

Ask one of these buyers to be a regular consultant for your restaurant—for a fee, of course. Perhaps periodic meetings with your service staff to teach them about the wines on your list can be scheduled. Identify this wine consultant on your wine list, adding credibility to your claims of good value.

When buying wine, for most restaurateurs it's not important how a wine will develop five or 10 years from now but rather how drinkable it is right now. There is a limit to how much capital you want to tie up in wines that might be excellent sometime in the future.

> *"We want our customers to know that we respect our business and that in turn engenders their respect for the bar."*
> **CRAIG TENNIS**
> Residuals
> Studio City,
> California

Offer a "consultant's selection" of fine wines at a 75 percent mark-up (less than your normal wine mark-ups). Tell the customers that these prices are only a few dollars more than the same wines cost at your consultant's store.

Reassured about the reasonableness of your pricing, knowledgable customers will buy your better wines and others will feel comfortable with the price of whatever they order.

If you are in a state that does not have independent wine stores, your task will be more difficult, but wine experts reside in every community. Perhaps the local newspaper or the local community college has a food and wine specialist.

Caveat: Many customers who enjoy wine with meals, also enjoy an after-meal cognac or liqueur. By all means, recommend an after-dinner drink as long as the customer is not in apparent danger of becoming intoxicated. It is important to determine who at the table is the driver, if the party is traveling by car. The server should be alert to how much alcohol this person consumes over the course of the meal so that driving ability is not impaired.

This may seem to be asking a lot from servers, but watch-dogging alcohol consumption is now part of the job. There are training programs available on this subject which should be mandatory for everybody on staff working directly with customers.

Wine, spirits, and beer are an enjoyable part of eating out for many of your customers. Responsible drinkers will appreciate your caring. Irresponsible drinkers urgently need your caring.

About Cognac

6) Most restaurateurs pour a one-and-a-half-ounce serving of cognac in a large snifter. The bigger the snifter, the more insignificant that one-and-a-half ounces seems. And cognac doesn't come cheap, so the higher the price, the smaller that pour looks.

Don't throw your large brandy snifters away. Use them instead for unusual specialty drinks and signature desserts. For cognac, use baby snifters and increase your pour to two or two-and-a-half ounces. Raise your price, but not proportionately, perhaps by 25 to 33 percent, more than enough to cover the increased pouring cost. Your customers will perceive an excellent value.

Smokers

7) They aren't pariahs. Most of them are very nice people. They may even be bigger spenders at restaurants than non-smokers. (A customer smoking a Macanudo after dinner will almost always have two cognacs while he's finishing that long cigar).

Today, virtually all restaurants designate non-smoking areas, but avoid dividing the dining room in such a way that it makes the smoker feel like a second-class citizen. A well-maintained, efficient heating, ventilat-

"If people want to call me Murph, let them. It's important to be flexible in this business."
ED HAWKINS
Murph's
Franklin Square,
New York

14

ing, and air-conditioning system will usually keep tobacco smoke well under control.

Cigar and pipe smokers really find life difficult in public areas. What a plus you could have by establishing a special "club" room where cigar and pipe smokers are welcome.

That kind of warm concern for all your guests is another way to help your customers perceive the value of your restaurant.

3

PRICE FOR PROFIT

There are times when you have to stand up to your accountant or financial advisor and say "Whoa." Except for chain operations, the restaurant business is not a formula business. There is no set-in-concrete equation for food and beverage costs, nor for most of the other costs you're going to encounter.

Traditional industry percentages as targets or guidelines? Yes, as long as you remember that they are only guidelines—and that the bottom line is making a profit.

Let's assume that menu prices are set up as mentioned in Chapter 2. Food cost percentages are higher for the more expensive items and lower for the less expensive ones, aiming for an average 40 percent overall food cost.

After a month, food costs are actually 45 percent. Red flag! Here's a quick checklist:

Have you been receiving all of the food you have been paying for?

Is food accurately portioned?

Is food thrown out because it has gone bad?

Do food checks match with the amount of food that has been depleted from storage?

> "Know accounting, so that every day you can put your finger on where the money is going."
> **CECELIA TALLICHET**
> Specialty Restaurants Anaheim, California

You may find your five percent overage from that exercise, pinpointing a continuing problem that you can now stem. But if this doesn't uncover the reason for the higher costs, analyze the food checks to see what customers are ordering and what check averages are.

This analysis may reveal that customers appreciate the value of the top-of-the-line items, with food costs of 50 percent, ordering proportionately more of them than anticipated, skewing preliminary estimates of overall food percentages.

Don't be tempted to raise prices to bring food cost percentages in line with what you originally programmed. Your customers may react by switching to lower priced entrees which can decrease your profits.

People can only eat one entree. Raising the price to $25 can cause a customer to switch from a $20 steak with a 50 percent food cost to a $14 sliced steak platter with a 45 percent food cost. That translates into $2.30 less profit on the entree alone. It escalates. Most people are uncomfortable spending more for a bottle of wine than they spend on the entree, so that customer will spend $6 less for wine, meaning $3 more is deducted from your profits.

And, of course, some customers will go to another restaurant, not telling you why. Your percentages are "coming into line" but profits are going to hell.

Instead of raising prices, analyze restaurant checks further. How many a la carte items are you selling? How many soups, appetizers, wines, or beers with the meal? How many desserts, after-dinner drinks?

For instance, if appetizers aren't selling, they might be over-priced, not by accountants' standards, but by your customers' standards.

> *"Profitability is determined by actual profit for each item, not relative food-cost percentages. Give me a $5 profit with a high cost percentage rather than a $3 profit with a low cost percentage every day."*
>
> **JIM ANDERSON**
> Oklahoma State University
> Stillwater, Oklahoma

17

Most people love shrimp cocktail, baked clams, clams on the half shell. But shellfish is expensive, even wholesale. Challenge price resistance by slashing your mark-ups on these items. Be satisfied with a $1 profit on each. That's a dollar more than you're getting from that customer now. Some restaurants in Salt Lake City even give a generous shrimp cocktail free with every entree, generating more business.

Look at the soups you offer. Are they really outstanding? Then why don't your customers order soup more often? It's probably not price, but quality, size of portion, and presentation. The late Percy Goodale made his small New York City restaurant's reputation on clam chowder and lobster stew. Not only were both soups of outstanding quality, but the waiter theatrically proffered each patron a bottle of Harvey's Bristol Cream Sherry and suggested a dollop in the soup. A perfect marriage of flavors, a perfect blend of memorable dish and presentation.

> *"The key to survival in the restaurant business is the ability to adapt and the use of marketing programs to maximize revenues."*
> **JAMES GRAZIADEI**
> The Fountain
> Chesapeake,
> Virginia

If your check analysis shows that desserts are moving slowly, it's also telling you that your staff is not "selling" desserts to the customers. Retrain the staff.

At Your Bar

People are drinking less, but ordering better brands. Help them choose. In Chapter 1, we spoke about the importance of using your back bar as a selling tool. Put a shelf up on your back bar with a prominent sign, "Millionaire's Club" or "Big Spenders' Brands" or something similar.

Display a variety of super-premium brands on this shelf, priced modestly enough to be an obvious value but still delivering a higher per-drink profit than the premium house brands that you pour.

Offer a better quality house wine. Bar managers seriously wonder, "Why should I pour an upscale white wine? My customers at the bar just want white wine to be cold, something to hold while they socialize and sip."

All too often true. But you are in Show Biz, remember?

You can put a much better white wine in the glass than most of your competitors and make the same per-glass profit at a price only 25 cents higher than the going rate. Let your customers know what you're giving them. Some will appreciate the improved flavor, some won't care, but no one will desert you over 25 cents.

> *"Wine by the glass is the best thing that ever happened to the restaurateur, to the distributor, and to your customer."*
> **KEVIN ZRALY**
> Windows on the World
> New York, New York

This also opens the subject of wine generally and gives your bartender an opportunity to suggest some step-up white wines, also by the glass. Up go your per-drink profits.

Remember, you don't bank percentages, you bank profits. Price your food and drinks to give you maximum profit per transaction while giving your customers high perceived value.

4

LEARN TO SELL

Everyone employed in your restaurant is a sales representative for you. It's important for the restaurant's success that they be good at it.

But very few restaurant employees—not many owners or managers, for that matter—think of themselves as salespeople. "Sell" is a four-letter word. They don't want to "sell" anything to their customers that the customers don't want.

You don't want that either, because that's not a professional approach. Professional sales representatives, whether they're selling machine tools or Tiffany jewels, thrive on repeat business and word of mouth. They sometimes establish long-lasting friendships with their customers.

A professional knows that selling is informing a prospective customer how a product can be useful, establishing that the price offers true value, asking for the order, and seeing that the product is delivered on time and in good condition. If follow-up service is needed, the professional is there.

Not any different from what should be happening in your restaurant. How do you

> *"Don't underestimate the importance of one-to-one marketing. Seek out your key customers, visit them, shake their hands, and ask for their business."*
> **DUANE J. MORRISON**
> The Pirates' House
> Savannah, Georgia

and your employees become professional salespeople?

Start with warmth. Like people, be able to smile, and be comfortable talking to strangers.

Know the product. How is the food prepared? What's in that dish? What does it taste like? If desserts aren't made on the premises, be informed about the supplier.

What wines would be suitable with different foods? Servers must know what the house wines are by name and type, not just "red, white, or rose?" They must be familiar with the difference between blended Scotch whiskies and single malt Scotch whiskies, the difference between VS and VSOP cognac, and just what is Armagnac?

"I'll ask the bartender" not only wastes time which is money, but conveys a message of incompetence that colors whatever food or drink recommendations the server subsequently offers.

How do your servers get so smart? It starts when you hire them. Select outgoing people who are willing to learn. Tell them that part of their job is to familiarize themselves with food and spirits in a reasonable period of time.

Then teach them.

Schedule regular training meetings. Some restaurateurs guarantee attendance at meetings by scheduling them on pay day, between the afternoon and evening shifts. Whatever works, but do pay the staff for training time. The chef can certainly handle instruction relating to food. Although specials are reviewed with the staff every day, at the weekly meetings the chef can go into detail on the subtleties of taste and the intricacies of preparation of a favorite house special.

> "We give a lot of attention to the food we serve, but we give even more attention to the service. If on one visit the food is only so-so, people will still return. But if the service is sub-par, they won't come back and they'll tell their friends not to bother."
>
> **TOM CLARY**
> Clary's American Grill
> Springfield, Missouri

The head bartender should be able to talk about spirits and specialty drinks. The staff can hear a short explanation about a different category of spirits each week. Outside experts may have to discuss wine. Suppliers can be helpful, unless you're in a state where you have to purchase wine through state stores.

Wherever you are located, an exceptional source of professional expertise can be found at two- and four-year colleges that offer restaurant management curricula.

> *"Recruit well, train well, pay well, and insist on total professionalism."*
> **NEIL S. REYER**
> Chemical Bank
> New York, New York

The professors teaching these courses frequently do double duty as consultants and can be very helpful at a reasonable cost.

You can also learn by reading restaurant trade magazines, some of the many books on this subject, and by personally talking to successful restaurateurs. In the next two sections of this book are the stories of over 40 successful restaurateurs.

Understand that you and your staff are in the same boat as the doctors, engineers, teachers, computer professionals, airline pilots, and countless others. You can never stop learning or you stagnate. There is no rest for the restaurateur.

5

ROPE AND TIE THE CUSTOMER

A restaurant needs a personality to set it apart and attract new customers. Residuals in Studio City, California, displays actual residual checks made out for less than $1 to performers who frequent the restaurant. A wallboard keeps track of where the show business regulars are working today.

The Garfield's restaurant chain pioneered white paper table covers and a glass of crayons on every table. That turned out to be surprisingly popular with teenagers and business people as well as the young families originally targeted.

In addition, restaurants need regular customers who can be counted on for enough weekly revenue to produce a profit. As this base of regulars expands, so do profits and the likelihood of long-term success.

To fill your new restaurant, you are going to have to convince people who are regulars at some other restaurant to switch to your place. Your success depends on it.

> *"Be unorthodox. Be different from others, not a me-too. Don't be afraid to break the rule-book cliches."*
> **VINCENT ORZA**
> Garfield's
> Restaurants
> Oklahoma City,
> Oklahoma

Who and where are these potential regulars?

From noon until 6 P.M., they're probably within the 10-minute circle. During the workday, few people care to spend more than 10 minutes traveling to a restaurant.

On a local map, draw a circle with a 10-minute traveling time radius and your location at the center. Find out what business firms, professionals, schools, hospitals, churches, funeral parlors, motels, hotels, theaters, and private homes are within that circle.

Seek out people who live or work inside this circle and ask them questions.

When eating out, what foods do they want for lunch? Between lunch and dinner? For dinner?

How late would they like to see the kitchen stay open?

What are their favorite foods, wines, spirits, beers?

What do they like in sports, music, general entertainment?

Do they need a meeting room occasionally or regularly?

Digest what you've learned and integrate it with the type of restaurant you want to run and the type of clientele you want to attract.

When your new menu implementing some of the suggestions made to you is ready, send a copy of it to all of the people you surveyed, thanking them for their suggestions (whether you used any of their ideas or not). Enclose a $25 gift certificate that can be used for food and/or drinks, no strings.

Once you've roped them, now you tie them.

When these or any customers walk through your door, pay attention. Greet them immediately. No matter how busy you

> *"When the staff meeting is over, I smile, straighten my tie, and announce, it's show time!"*
> **VINCENT BOMMARITO**
> Tony's
> St. Louis, Missouri

are, at least say, "Welcome, I'll be right with you." Return as quickly as possible to seat them or direct them to the bar.

Dining room customers appreciate attentive service but don't want to feel rushed. After requesting cocktail orders, ask if they are on a tight schedule and personally expedite their service if the answer is yes. In no case, however, should the server present the check until it is requested. Some customers would be offended and it certainly squelches the opportunity to sell dessert or an after-dinner drink. Even the party in a hurry might have gotten such fast service that there is time for dessert.

When customers want to leave, they will signal or try to signal their server. Don't let your servers exemplify the old joke, "God finally caught his eye." Servers, captains, hosts, management, and owners should constantly be alert to any attempt at communication from a customer. At Phil Lehr's Steakery in San Francisco an attractive beacon on every table can be turned on to request service.

Customers at your bar appreciate receiving a first drink promptly. Given a choice of refilling a drink or greeting and serving a newcomer, bartenders should assure the sitting customer the refill is on the way and attend to the newcomer immediately.

The cocktail hour, from about 4 P.M. to 7 P.M., offers your best opportunity to develop new lunch and dinner customers. A cardinal rule in selling is that it is easier and less expensive to increase sales to existing customers than to make a sale to a stranger.

When you are newly in business, most of the people coming into the lounge have not eaten in your restaurant. So instead of the trite assortment of happy hour food that most restaurants offer, have a server circu-

> *"The restaurant business can be pictured as an inverted pyramid. The customers are at the top supported by descending layers of staff, mid-management, top management, and owners. Everybody in the organization has a responsibility to the customer. Management must support the staff."*
>
> **BEIRNE BROWN**
> Cuisine Management
> Naples, Florida

lating through the lounge describing and offering bite-size samples of some of the menu items. Over the course of three hours, tastes of four or five specialties might be offered.

Later, pass around miniature copies of the lunch and dinner menus.

Try two Surprise Nights every week (not announcing which nights until the last minute). Give everybody in the lounge a ticket and at 6 P.M., 7 P.M., and 8 P.M. have the bartender call out a number. The winning number receives a free lunch or dinner (for one only—maybe paying friends will join the winner), but the holder of the number must be present when the number is called to collect. Keep drawing until there's a winner.

Start a 5 P.M. to 8 P.M. Club. Every time a club member visits your lounge during those hours, punch a card. A card with 30 punches can be redeemed for a free lunch, 45 punches for a free dinner. Think of it as a frequent-flyer type of program.

Dinner business can be further expanded when you think of dinner hours as multiple personality time. Early dinners are frequently attractive to older people and to families with young children. Offer an early-bird menu, perhaps even starting before 5 P.M., with smaller portions at lower prices. Include popular lunch items at the lunch price until 7 P.M., when normal dinner hours generally begin.

After 7 P.M., dinner patrons generally don't appreciate loud music. Quiet background music or a pianist playing softly sets a pleasant mood. Offer signature menu items such as Vic Giannotti's Eight-finger Cavatelli or Eamonn Doran's Gaelic Steak.

> *"If you want to be in business five years from now, you have to get involved with your customers. My basic premise is that I'm in business to give my customers what they want— including a staff that understands that the word 'no' is taboo."*
> **EAMONN DORAN**
> Eamonn Doran's
> New York, New York

Develop new business from lounge customers, work for repeat business from restaurant patrons, and since you can draw from an expanded 30-minute traveling radius for dinner customers, create an advertising program that reaches out to everyone living within that larger circle.

Late dinner hours draw customers with different needs. They may be coming from a movie, a ball game, a trip, from a long day at work, or perhaps they've been socializing in your lounge and decided to have something to eat.

They probably won't want the same full meal as your regular dinner customers, so in addition to showing them your dinner menu, trot out a "supper" menu. It can be based on the lunch or early-bird menu.

If you don't want to maintain a kitchen staff in the late hours, devise a menu that floor or bar staff can handle, either directly from the refrigerator (a double shrimp cocktail) or light entrees that can be readied in the microwave.

You can also pre-portion roast beef, pastrami, or corned beef for overstuffed deli sandwiches that can be served cold or warmed in the microwave.

> *"The challenge for a restaurant located off the beaten track is to convince tonight's customers to come back."*
> **BERN LAXER**
> Bern's Steak House
> Tampa, Florida

Keeping Customers Loyal

They love you, you're filling the restaurant, you're a success. Now if you don't rock the boat you can keep banking profits for the rest of your life, or at least until the lease runs out.

Wrong.

Just as friends or spouses become boring, restaurants lose their appeal. There's always another new, interesting place that needs to be checked out. Isn't that how you attracted your regulars? Lured from restaurants that had their loyalty until they discovered your place.

Don't let your customers take your restaurant for granted.

Daily specials are not a panacea. To really create an aura of excitement, open yourself to what's going on in the world, nearby and distant.

What's happening now? Is there a World's Fair being planned or celebrated? If yes (isn't there always a World's Fair being planned or celebrated?), then feature a promotion celebrating that city's food and drink specialties.

> "I learned that a restaurant is like theater. Once the curtain is up, there's no stopping the play."
> **ELIZABETH TERRY**
> Elizabeth on 37th
> Savannah, Georgia

Costume your staff to reflect the city's culture and hang posters (available from airlines or tourist offices). Involve local merchants—travel agent, supermarket, wine store, newspaper, radio station—and jointly sponsor a contest for an expenses-paid trip for two to the World's Fair.

Is this an America's Cup challenge year? An Olympics year?. A presidential election year? Do some research and create innovative ways for your restaurant to celebrate these events with customers.

February is traditionally slow for restaurateurs. Dedicate that month to romance. If you want inspiration,visit The Madonna Inn in San Luis Obispo, California, a monument to romance that is nationally known.

If you want to attract singles, recreate Sadie Hawkins Week as it was celebrated on college campuses in the 1940s and '50s. There's a generation or two that never heard of Al Capp's Lil' Abner and the zany citizens of Dogpatch, U.S.A. In Dogpatch, Sadie Hawkins Day was the one day a year when girls chased boys, marrying the one they caught.

Night Lounge Business

Your restaurant can't be all things to all people. Don't even try. But a late-night lounge will probably attract different types of crowds on different nights.

A sing-along piano bar might lure dining room customers into remaining in the lounge on Friday and Saturday nights, while also attracting a crowd coming from dinner elsewhere.

Monday night football and other sports events on TV might attract Sunday through Thursday night business if you add incentives such as special beer prices or free hot dogs or trivia contests.

For otherwise slow sports nights, use a VCR to create unique sports draws. In the days leading up to a championship boxing match, schedule some evenings for showing videotapes of memorable boxing matches past. Copy Eamonn Doran's and import videotapes of overseas championship soccer or rugby matches, probably something other places near you won't be offering.

Supply the physical education or audio-visual departments at local high schools and colleges with blank video tapes for putting together highlight videos of their athletic teams. Periodically invite team members and their families to off-hours screening of the video at your place. Provide pitchers of soda for the kids and special drink prices and munchies for the adults.

Videotape your own special events, Halloween parties, St. Patrick's Day, New Year's Eve, and edit the tape into a fast-paced video. Spread the word that you'll be running that video continuously on your TV screens all week (but without sound, so other customers won't be disturbed).

> *"We have to communicate to people that when they come to our restaurant they will enjoy themselves. The restaurant business isn't just about serving good food. We're on stage and our patrons want a good show."*
>
> **PETER PRATT**
> Pratt's Inn
> Yorktown Heights,
> New York

At the end of the year, edit a highlights tape and have a Best of Last Year Party on the Sunday after the Super Bowl.

Don't take yourself and your restaurant too seriously. Food, drink, and service are serious concerns in the restaurant business, of course, but so are good times. If your customers don't think you're having fun, they're not going to have fun.

6

KEEP THINGS LIVELY

If the heads of your customers were transparent, you could view streams of thought about what they want in a restaurant: Excitement, pleasant surprises, new experiences. Entertainment, camaraderie, attention. Good food, good wine, good drink, good service.

In the real world, what's hardest to find? Excitement, pleasant surprises, and new experiences.

Here's your opportunity to shine. Let's use some imagination.

The biggest category for book sales is cookbooks. Count the number of cookbooks that local bookstores offer for sale. Or how many different cookbooks were published in the last five years. Or how many different recipes were published in magazines and the weekly food sections of newspapers last month alone.

Does that suggest that Americans are entranced with food? With unique recipes?

Hundreds of people regularly write or broadcast restaurant reviews for every type of media, from major metropolitan dailies, national magazines, and television network

"People dine with their eyes—plain and drab, you missed the boat. Dazzle your patrons when they walk through the door. Then give them good service and reward your top selling waiters and waitresses."
BOB McCAIN
Jonathan's
Orlando, Florida

31

affiliates to local pennysavers and rural radio stations.

Forbes Magazine, a serious financial journal, is equally serious about reviewing restaurants.

Are Americans interested in restaurants?

Newspapers regularly report on wine, often with weekly columns in addition to seasonal features. Many magazines devote sizable editorial space to wine and the most successful liquor and wine retailers devote major portions of their floor space to wine displays.

Is wine important to many Americans?

Put all of these interests together—food, wine, and restaurants—and come up with a new experience for your customers that will give them excitement and surprises.

For instance:

Pick a city—any city. New Orleans?

Borrow or buy every book available about New Orleans restaurants and collect recipes for food and cocktails popular there. Plan a month-long celebration, culminating in a party that celebrates Mardi Gras for 10 days preceding Ash Wednesday.

Recreate the atmosphere and food specialties of top New Orleans restaurants, perhaps Brennan's for week one, Paul Prudhomme's K-Paul for week two, Commander's Palace for week three and a selection of Louisiana specialties from many of the other fine restaurants for week four.

During the entire month feature oysters on the half shell and traditional drinks such as Pat O'Brien's Hurricane, the Sazerac cocktail, and a Cajun Mary. Plus Dixieland bands, Dixieland bands, Dixieland bands.

Kick this gala off with a preview party the day before the promotion officially begins. Invite the local media and your VIP list (your better customers and local celebrities) to a 4

> *"Restaurants have guests, not customers. Banks have customers. The service staff has to project that image of hospitality: be happy, look and feel healthy, and feel terrific. Then the guest will be happy, healthy and leave feeling terrific."*
>
> **TOM KELLY**
> Cornell University School of Hotel Administration
> Ithaca, New York

P.M. to 6 P.M. buffet featuring New Orleans food and an open bar featuring New Orleans drinks.

Liven things up with a Dixieland band that plays through the evening. Let the open bar begin charging regular prices for drinks at 6 P.M. Many of the party guests will stay on and spend some money. Open the party room to regular customers for the rest of the evening.

Another idea.

A month-long celebration of France, using the same basic approach. Start this on Bastille Day, July 14. Instead of a preview party, hand-deliver picnic baskets filled with French bread, Brie cheese, French pate, and (where legal) a bottle of French wine to key people at local newspapers, TV and radio stations, other media people in your market and to your VIP customer list. Include information on all of the upcoming month's activities at your restaurant to celebrate French cooking, French wines, and French restaurants.

Perhaps Foods and Wines From France, the French Government Tourist Office, or Air France will help you with this promotion.

Read to get ideas. Read restaurant trade magazines such as *Restaurant Business, Restaurant Hospitality, Restaurants and Institutions, Food Arts, FoodService Product News, Cheers, Top Shelf* and *Nation's Restaurant News* and specialized consumer magazines such as *Gourmet, Bon Appetit,* and *Food and Wine.*

Ask your supplier salesmen for ideas and information on available merchandising help.

> *"We made a mistake. Sugar is added to the brew and we accidentally put in double the normal amount. This meant a big head which took time to settle before we could serve it, but the taste was outstanding. The mistake became our standard, Charleys Cream Ale."*
>
> **MARTIN TWIST**
> Charleys
> Louisville, Kentucky

7

NETWORK YOUR SUPPLIERS

Suppliers can be your best friends and even good customers if you give them the chance.

Talk to all of the sales representatives calling on you. Be at least as gracious to suppliers and possible suppliers as you are to your customers.

What should you expect from your suppliers?

"The restaurant business is a fantasy. People coming into this business should have enough capital to pay for their mistakes."

PETER PRATT
Pratt's Inn
Yorktown Heights,
New York

- Reliability.
- Knowledge about the product.
- Fair prices.
- Promotional information.
- Complete information on advertising and marketing support planned in your area for products you now buy or intend to buy.
- Immediate access to new products.
- A knowledge of your business.
- An interest in your business and your needs.
- Ideas on how you can increase your profits.

What suppliers can expect from you

- Consideration of their problems. For instance, delivery costs are high. Order as much at one time as is possible without affecting freshness.
- Prompt payment.
- Courtesy. If a sales representative calls at an inconvenient time, suggest a more propitious time. Don't keep salespeople waiting needlessly, or treat them condescendingly. Don't let middle management or floor staff take out their frustrations on salespeople calling on you. This is both unacceptable behavior and atrocious business. Anybody who enters your restaurant is a potential customer. Make a good impression. Why?

Your sales representative has bosses, co-workers, family, and friends. All of them eat in restaurants.

The companies that provide suppliers with the products that are sold to you have sales forces. Those salespeople eat in restaurants.

Tell your suppliers that they are valued partners. Extend to all of their employees a "Partners Card" good for a discount on food and beverages whenever they visit your restaurant.

Ask your new "partners" for the names, addresses, and product lines of the salespeople who call on them.

Write these salespeople, describing your restaurant and mentioning how you are using their products. Welcome any suggestions they might have on how existing or new products can improve what you now offer.

Brag about your restaurant. Include menus. Welcome them to lunch or dinner

"If you are thinking of yourself as a non-working investor, don't expect to make a big profit on your investment. In fact, if you just want to be part owner of a restaurant, don't invest in one that has to start from scratch. Find a good restaurant owned by people who know what they are doing. Invest enough money with them so that they can blossom and you'll be helping to make a 'success' happen. "

TOM SLATTERY
Manhattan Restaurant Association
New York, New York

the next time they are in your area. Mention meeting facilities if you have any. Compliment the local supplier and your own sales representative if appropriate. Send copies of the letters to the suppliers and representatives mentioned.

It's called networking. Good things will happen.

8

ADVERTISE EFFECTIVELY

Start by creating a mailing list.

Tell customers that you appreciate their business and would like to remember them on special occasions. Ask for birthdays (year of birth not necessary), anniversaries, names and birthdays of other family members, dates of particular importance.

A week before the special event, mail an appropriate card and promise a present on the customer's next visit.

Computers make this easy.

Have a number of gifts in inventory from which you can make a thoughtful selection. For instance, a fragrance can be attractively packaged with your restaurant's logo at a very reasonable cost. You can find sources for this or other suitable gifts at the National Restaurant Association Show in Chicago every May, the International Hotel and Motel Show in New York every November, or at some of the major regional shows. Your state restaurant associations will have dates and locations.

Develop a newsletter to give your customers reasons to stop in more frequently.

"My advice to anybody now in the restaurant business or planning to enter it is to get computer savvy."
CARL CARBONE
Carbone's/
Gaetano's
Hartford,
Connecticut

Perhaps include a recipe for one of your more appetizing offerings to encourage recipients to keep your newsletter on hand as does Wesley's restaurants in Virginia Beach, Virginia, and Greenwich, Connecticut.

Develop a theme that appears in promotional pieces and advertising. Make a simple statement and repeat it often until it immediately brings your restaurant to mind. For example, everyone in New York knows that the Russian Tea Room is "just slightly to the left of Carnegie Hall."

Question your customers.

Where do they hear about other restaurants that they frequent? What restaurant reviewers do they read and respect? When they read a restaurant ad, what information is most important to them? What publication did they see that ad in? If they hear an ad for a restaurant on the radio, what was said that makes them want to visit that place? What radio station did they hear it on?

Keep notes. When enough interviews are completed to give you a cross-section of response from customers who epitomize the customers you want to attract, analyze and study the results.

Place your advertising in the media that is most favored, stressing the points about your restaurant that this research indicates will elicit the strongest response from your target audience.

This approach is not foolproof, but one intelligent way to start an ad campaign. A good rule is to give an advertising program time to work. You are not going to work miracles with one ad. You may not even get a measurable response until two or three months have passed.

> *"The Casablanca Syndrome can be very destructive to the victim's pocketbook. Regular customers frequently see the owners mingling, smiling or laughing, telling jokes, talking sports—and they see Rick. This is the way to live—eat, drink and be merry and get well paid for it, is what many of them think. Reality is quite different."*
>
> **LOUIS MAGUIRE**
> Ryan McFadden's/
> Cafe Maguire
> New York, New York

Don't panic. Do keep records of any results you get. When new customers come in ask them how they heard of you and keep a record. If at the end of 13 weeks you're getting positive results or comments on the advertising, renew the media that generate those results for another 13 weeks. This applies even when the business attracted doesn't cover the costs of the advertising.

The impact of advertising is cumulative. As long as you see some response, that impact should grow through repetition of your message. If it doesn't after about six to nine months, then change the medium or the message.

If you are located near motels, consider advertising in the AAA travel guides. Motels get a lot of business from the AAA guides. Go after these customers with a small ad.

If there are major hotels in the area, consider advertising in the entertainment publications distributed in their rooms or at the concierge's desk.

Definitely place an ad in the local telephone company Yellow Pages. People consult the Yellow Pages and when they do, they are ready to spend money. Don't overlook the catering section or the restaurant guide section if there is one.

Remember, you not only want to reach out and touch someone, you want to hook them into being a loyal patron of your restaurant.

Coming up: case histories of restaurants that did just that.

> *"I like to introduce a waiter to his customers as 'the world famous waiter'. When they say famous for what?, I answer, 'impeccable service', and leave the waiter to live up to it. It always works."*
>
> **TED BALESTRERI**
> The Sardine Factory
> Monterey,
> California

Part II

SUCCESS STORIES

9

WINDOWS' WIZARD OF WINE

Windows on the World, located at the top of New York's World Trade Center, is virtually a universe of its own. It includes The Restaurant, the main dining salon with 350 seats, open from 5 P.M. to 10 P.M. every day, noon to 7:30 P.M. on Sunday. Before 5, The Restaurant functions as The Club, a private membership luncheon club.

The Cellar in the Sky is the wine cellar for the entire Windows complex. With 36 seats and one 7:30 P.M. sitting, Monday through Saturday, The Cellar also offers a spectacular prix fixe dinner designed around five wines.

The Hors d'Oeuvrerie and the Statue of Liberty Lounge with 240 seats offer conventional breakfasts Monday through Friday, Sunday brunch, and from 3 P.M. to 1 A.M. every day (midnight on Sundays), a selection of appetizers from around the world. There are also two function rooms seating up to 1,175 and the City Lights Bar, described as "a thousand-bottle liquor library," with 76 kinds of gin and 130 different Scotches, open from 3 P.M. daily, from noon on weekends.

Kevin Zraly was hired in 1976 to create the wine list for this sprawling entity. With a budget in the millions, he personally tasted and evaluated thousands of wines to come up with his original 700 selections. In the process, he developed an excellent sense of the wine market—when to buy and what quantities to buy to lock in the best values.

By 1983, wine sales had reached $2 million annually. By 1988, they had ratcheted up to $3 million.

42

"At first, I had a formula for pricing the wines that precisely reduced the percentage of mark-up as our cost for a particular wine increased," said Zraly. "But I have learned that this is a mistake."

"Today's customers are very much into wine and consider wine selection, service, and pricing to be as important as food and atmosphere. Still, the great majority are insecure about their knowledge and make their selection from the right side of the wine list. To them, a $30 wine is twice as good as a $15 bottle.

"They buy the trendy wines—75 percent of our wine sales are from 40 wines, while we have over 700 wines on our master wine list," Zraly added. "So we'll mark these 40 wines up two-and-a-half to three times our cost.

"For the knowledgeable customer we offer remarkable wines with much more modest mark-ups. They realize the value and appreciate it."

It's one thing to acquire 700 different wines to offer. It's quite another to sell them well enough to build annual sales to more than $3 million in just over a decade.

"When we opened the restaurant, I asked my boss who was going to help me sell wine to customers," Zraly remembered. "I got a one-word answer: 'You'."

Zraly realized he would have to clone himself quickly.

He began an eight-week training course for captains and waiters. He scheduled wine school on weekly pay days from 3:30 to 4:30 P.M., convenient to both shifts.

The first session covered the basics of proper wine etiquette and good service. Among the lessons, that champagne corks are never popped, the difference between pouring a red wine versus a white, precisely where to cut the lead with the corkscrew, and when to properly remove the cork from the table.

More subtle, but just as important to robust wine sales, is the psychology of presentation. Zraly's advice to staff included:

1) Expect customers to order wine.

2) Help them feel comfortable about ordering.

3) Be positive. Don't ask negative questions like, "You don't want any wine, do you?" or even, "Do you want wine?" Ask instead, "Which wine have you chosen for dinner?", "Would you like Chenin Blanc or Riesling with your trout?", "May I suggest our special wine of the month with your entree?"

4) Know when to take wine to the table. Immediately!

5) Know how to present wine. Professionally!

6) Know when to refill wine glasses. When almost empty.

The following weeks had the staff studying white wines from California in more depth, white wines of Burgundy, wines of Bordeaux, German and Italian wines, and champagnes and sparkling wines.

Today, the training includes learning about wines from Australia and Long Island, as well as exceptional wines being produced in other parts of the U. S. and around the world. At every meeting, the wines discussed are tasted.

After the training course was completed, monthly refresher meetings focused on wine selling techniques, making intelligent recommendations to customers, and tasting wines new to the restaurant. The staff soon did such a remarkable job of presenting and selling wine with confidence that members of the private luncheon club wanted to know how they had learned so much.

Club members besieged Zraly to teach them, too. The class for interested club members quickly expanded to include friends. A year later, it had become so popular that the public was invited to participate.

Now five wine classes a year (one night a week for eight weeks) are offered. Each enrolls 100 students at $400 per. Classes are sold out three months in advance.

Attendees frequently dine in one of the restaurants either before or after class, bringing considerable business to Windows On The World. Graduates also schedule the facilities of the restaurant for private wine tastings for social or business occasions.

The success of the wine school led Zraly to write *The Complete Windows On The World Wine Course*. Not a wine textbook, but what Zraly calls "the Windows On The World Wine School between two covers," it has sold over 250,000 copies and was recently updated for the fifth time. Published by Sterling Publishing Co. in New York, it is available directly from Windows On The World or at bookstores for $21.95.

Keep Marketing

"You have to keep marketing. If you sit back, it's not going to work," said Zraly.

A marketing executive's dream since opening day is Cellar in the Sky, the 36-seat "restaurant within the restaurant."

"Every two weeks our chef creates an outstanding seven-course meal. We select five different wines as accompaniments.

44

Reservations for the single sitting on Thursday, Friday, or Saturday nights are sold out at least a month ahead of time. Monday through Wednesday are completely booked but with shorter waiting periods.

"A fixed menu, a fixed price of $80 with a $20 deposit on reservation—people are gladly waiting for their turns," said Zraly. "Further proof that customers want to experiment with food and wine match-ups.

"Even so, Cellars just breaks even. But it is very important to our total operation because it allows us to showcase the talents of our chef and his staff, and the skills of the wine experts who taste and select the wines for our extensive list."

In his normal duties as cellarmaster, Alec Brough will taste over 1,000 wines in the course of a year. With the assistance of interested staff members, including captains and waiters, from five to 15 people will blind taste about 20 wines each week.

These wines are graded by category within similar price ranges. The main purpose is to detect those wines that are unsuitable.

Suppliers can receive the scores and comments given all wines, not just their own. They appreciate the open and capable evaluations, both to pinpoint any problems and evaluate the opportunities to intensify sales efforts.

"Our suppliers are our partners," Brough remarked . "Information sharing should be a two-way street."

"We take wine very seriously," added Zraly. "The wine program (including wine tours and book sales) is responsible for 20 to 25 percent of the total business done by Windows on the World."

Wine by the glass is one of the program's most promising components.

"My advice to anybody opening a new restaurant is to realize that wine by the glass is the best thing that ever happened to the restaurateur, to the distributor, and to your customer," Zraly said.

"It's not necessary to invest in a nitrogen system immediately. Begin modestly by offering good quality house wines plus a choice of two premium white wines and one premium red wine. These will move quickly enough that they won't spoil.

"If you expand your selections, as we have, you will probably do well to invest in a nitrogen system.

"Customers at lunch respond well to being able to get a good wine by the glass. We don't promote this at dinner, where most customers are comfortable with a full bottle. Sometimes, not wanting a second full bottle, they request a glass of the same wine they just finished or something similar.

"If you build a good wine-by-the-glass business at lunch, you may find distributors offering you some opportune buys. They know that your by-the-glass volume can quickly move a lot of cases of good quality wine when it is priced right.

"Everybody wins," Zraly promised. "And that is what makes this business fun, as well as profitable."

Planning Special Events

Also fun, albeit lots of work, are events like Passport to Lyon, a two-week promotion that began on the eve of Bastille Day (July 14) one year. The Hors d'Oeuvrerie offered a selection of seven hot and cold appetizers, two desserts, two aperitifs, two white wines, and two red wines, using recipes Executive Chef Karl Schmidt had collected during an earlier trip to Lyon.

Co-sponsor for the event was American Airlines, eager to showcase its new direct service between New York and Lyon. Every Windows guest was invited to enter a grand drawing for a deluxe trip for two to Lyon. The first prize was round-trip first-class air transportation, accommodations at the Grand Hotel Concorde, and complimentary car rental from Hertz.

The airlines had already proved themselves a rich resource. Earlier promotions were the Challenge of Sacher Tortes from Austria co-sponsored by Austrian Airways, and a Taste of Switzerland co-sponsored by SwissAir, which featured former White House chef Henry Haller as a guest speaker.

Less dramatic but with lasting effect was the week when in addition to the regular menus, a "Heartful Breakfast" was offered at the Hors d'Oeuvrerie, and the other Windows On The World restaurants offered a "Heartful Lunch."

The prix fixe lunch presented a choice of two appetizers, two entrees, and two desserts, every item labeled with calorie count, grams of fat, grams of saturated fat, and milligrams of cholesterol.

The low-cholesterol breakfast dishes were granola with dried blueberries, buckwheat pancakes with strawberry compote, and turkey hash with onions, peppers and potatoes.

Now an annual event, the Heartful meals were a tie-in with CountDOWN USA: The National Blood Pressure and Cholesterol Check. CountDOWN was sponsored by Voluntary Hospitals of America, Inc. a national network of 662 locally owned, not-for-profit hospitals and 172 affiliates.

CountDOWN USA intended to focus attention on the causes of heart disease and stroke and to encourage individuals at risk to change their behavior. Recipes were developed in cooperation with Voluntary Hospitals of America, Abbott Diagnostics, Dr. Susan Wilt of New York's Columbia Presbyterian Medical Center, and chef Schmidt.

The program was so popular that it is now an annual event and heart-healthy dishes have been added permanently to the breakfast menu.

SERVE WINE LIKE WINDOWS ON THE WORLD

All wine is served from the right side.

Glasses are placed over the dinner knife, white wine first. The red wine glass stands above and to the left of the white wine glass.

The wine should be opened and served before the food is served.

Bring the wine to the table and show it to the host. Say the name of the wine and the vintage aloud. This is the opporunity to clear up any mistakes. Pronunciation should be cleared with the steward.

Always open still wines on a solid surface like the table. White wines can be opened in the wine bucket. Don't open the bottle holding it in the air.

Cut the lead with the corkscrew knife below the lip so that the wine won't touch the lead as it's poured.

Wipe the top of the bottle with a side towel.

Insert the point of the corkscrew into the center of the cork and screw in until the entire coil is in the cork.

Hold the metal clamp against the bottle with one hand and lift up the lever with the other.

Don't pop the cork. When it's almost out, gently rock the cork from side to side to ease it out slowly.

Remove the cork and place it next to the glass.

Hold the bottle in your hand with the label facing the host.

Pour the host a two-ounce taste for approval. Rotate the bottle slightly when lifting to prevent dripping.

After the host approves, serve the eldest woman first, then the other women, always clockwise. If the table is very large or awkwardly placed, use your judgement about who should be served first, but still serve clockwise. Always pour the host last, even when the host is a hostess.

Fill white wine glasses half full, red wine glasses 1/3 full.

Remove the cork from the table after everyone is served.

A bottle of red wine is placed in the center of the table. Bottles of white wine belong in a bucket filled with ice water. The bucket should be placed next to the table and covered with a side towel folded lengthwise.

Never put an empty white wine bottle upside down in a bucket.

When bringing out a second bottle, always offer the host an opportunity to taste it before pouring. Use a new glass.

Champagne

Always open champagne bottles on a flat surface away from the table.

Remove the foil covering the wire cage around the cork.

Place your thumb or the palm of your hand firmly over the cork before removing the wire.

Loosen the wire cage while maintaining downward pressure on the cork.

Place an open side towel over the bottle and grasp it firmly.

Begin twisting the cork back and forth. The pressure will push the cork out slowly. When almost out, twist it over sideways and there will be no pop. Never pop the cork!

Pour slowly, against the side of the glass, to avoid excess bubbles.

10

RUNNING A TIGHT SHIP

On a visit to a wine cellar in St. Moritz, Switzerland in 1959, Dante Stephensen began collecting ideas for the restaurant he would one day open. Over the next 11 years, with visits to existing sailing ships, nautical lounges and other hideaways, the folder of ideas grew but nothing exactly caught the atmosphere for which he was looking.

"Then I realized that the secret was to build a ship not as it actually was, but the way people think it used to be," he explained. "In March of 1969, I gathered together a group of very talented men to recreate the romance of an 18th- century sailing frigate tied to a wharf and in late 1970 opened Dante's Down The Hatch in Underground Atlanta."

Polished wood and polished brasses highlighted the Ship's dining room, while more weathered (but still seaworthy) wood decorated the Wharf lounge.

For 11 years the restaurant flourished until Underground Atlanta itself succumbed in 1981. Stephensen moved his restaurant to suburban Buckhead, where it successfully operates today. He returned to the new Underground Atlanta when it reopened in 1989, occupying the site of his earlier restaurant. He had mothballed in place the original ship and other structures.

"Before entering the restaurant business I gave considerable thought to what qualities a restaurant needs to be successful," Stephensen said. "Twenty years later these necessary characteristics remain the same."

1) Quality of drink
2) Quality of food
3) Quality of entertainment
4) Interesting and genuine decor
5) Employees knowledgable, efficient and caring.
6) Trafficability, e.g., comfortable lighting, use of levels, traffic patterns for patrons in the restaurant.

How have each of these qualities been built into Dante's Down. The Hatch Restaurants?

1) The menu tells patrons that Dante pours 1 1/4 ounces of 'call-brand' quality liquors in all drinks, and the brands are named. The menu also lists 17 non-alcoholic "Drinks For Designated Drivers."

2) "If you can't prepare every item on your menu by yourself, sooner or later your chef will walk all over you," Stephensen declared, "so I selected a limited menu of items I both liked and could prepare."

Fondue dinners, salads, soups, Tasmanian Beef Stu and cheese trays highlight the Underground Atlanta menu, along with ice cream, chocolate fudge cake, pecan pie and cheesecake (homemade New York style by his 85-year-old Danish mother).

At the suburban Buckhead location, he has added steamed artichoke, homemade, handmade dumplings and chocolate fondue."Fondue, wine and cheese are European ideas that help create a fantasy trip for our customers," he said. "And it's worked for 20 years."

3) For the past 20 years, the Paul Mitchell Trio has nightly played nostalgia jazz, music not confined to an era or location, in the Ship's dining area, while folk singing and classical guitar greet the customers in the Wharf Lounge area of the restaurant.

4) The 18th-century ship decor has been supplemented with empty wine bottles hanging by their necks from the ceiling in the Wharf Lounge. Personal notes from customers who had ordered those bottles to celebrate a special occasion are inserted into them after they are washed. Frequently, customers also sign the labels.

5) See "Dignity, Integrity amd Profit Sharing," on page 11.

6) Trafficability means recognizing that when people go out for an evening to a nightclub or restaurant, they want to be seen. Restaurant design should take that into account. Attractive, open paths should be planned between the entrance and the tables,

and the rest rooms and the tables, with steps appropriately situated to allow for "entrances" by women.

"To these qualities I would add, 'Be visible in your restaurant'," said Stephensen. "I spend time at both Dante Down The Hatch restaurants every night, bouncing from table to table to bar, enthusiastically talking to customers.

"Enthusiasm is contagious. If I'm having fun, my employees and customers get caught up in it and everyone is soon having fun. And that's what keeps customers coming back...20 years worth."

DIGNITY, INTEGRITY AND PROFIT SHARING

Dante Stephensen's philosophy is that employees are family.

"Dante strives for all of the employees to be part of a team," said bartender/waitress Ellen Evans, "helping each other, not trying to beat the system but working together to build profits for maximum bonuses.

"He has two season box seats for the Atlanta Braves baseball games and employees can sign up for particular games. The names drawn out of a hat get the tickets. He has also spent extraordinary amounts of time to help a number of employees who ran into personal hardships."

"Restaurant people are pleasers. I'm not going to take advantage of them," Stephensen affirmed. "I don't hire just bodies. I hire a nucleus of good people who will attract other good people. I demand dignity and integrity. I also have nine profit-sharing plans that go all the way from the dishwashers to the managers."

Stephensen separates the bonus plans for managers from those for hourly employees so that managers are not tempted to enrich themselves at the expense of others.

All employees with Dante's for more than one year are eligible for bonuses in years when the restaurant shows a profit. Bartenders and cooks may also receive quarterly bonuses based primarily on cost savings. Costs are tracked by the month for key menu and key bar items, and objectives are established for each item. Actual costs are compared to desired costs and shift bonuses are determined. Members of each shift receive a share of the bonus, prorated to hours worked.

Where the profit could have been higher, the staff is told how much bigger the bonus would have been, providing an incentive to try harder next quarter to control costs. Workers are also quick to straighten out peers who goof off or steal since that actually deprives the staff of extra earnings.

Waiters and waitresses don't have individual banks. All checks are processed by the cashier, who can earn a bonus as high as $12.50 a day based on how well the checks balance at the end of the night. As a result, the restaurant seldom shows a shortage.

Integral to the year-end bonuses are individual management reviews of each employee's performance. Five managers evaluate each employee, all employees anonymously evaluate all other employees and each employee does a self-evaluation. The critiques are shared, but the individuals remain anonymous. Surprisingly, few feel resentment about comments by their peers.

"Dante cross-trains all of us so that one day I could be a bartender, another day a hostess or a waitress and sometimes I'll help in the kitchen," explained Ellen Evans. "This keeps the job interesting, but I'm not going to be equally proficient at each assignment. That's where the annual peer review helps me. Management can't see everything I do, but somebody working with me can."

When three managers sat with her to analyze her peer reviews, Evans was surprised that some employees felt she was unnecessarily brusque on occasion. Reflecting on this, she realized that when it was very busy she would work quickly without much small talk. Her associates took that as a slight. She resolved to work at being more aware of others' feelings no matter how hectic it got.

"Managers grade employees on 10 items," reported controller Gayle Palmer. "They are:
  *Disposition and personality
  *Willingness to pitch in without being asked
  *Success as a team player
  *Ability to deal with constructive criticism
  *Ability to handle crises
  *Grooming and dress
  *How much of a pain in the neck to schedule

*Ability to anticipate when extraordinary effort is required and then rise to meet the challenge

*Punctuality

*Degree of job cross-training and willingness to accept varying assignments.

"The employee then grades himself by the same criteria," Palmer continued. "Copies of all of these reviews are then given to the employee along with a letter from Stephensen telling the employee that Dante's basic questions are: '...do you achieve for us what I feel you are capable of achieving? When the day comes that you leave us, will you be fondly remembered or will your peers and managers feel, or say, good riddance? How are you regarded by our customers? How do you fit into our team?'"

"It's a lot of work for everybody, but our employees like the program and believe it's fair," Palmer added.

"The bonus is gravy," said Ellen Evans, "and makes it possible for me to plan exotic vacations. This is the first place I've ever worked that paid bonuses."

11

BIBA MIRRORS ITS CHEF/OWNER

Lydia Shire cherishes some time-honored American practices that she feels are disappearing from today's restaurants.

"I enjoy organ meats such as calves brains, tripe and chicken livers," she recounted. "While I understand that pipe and cigar smoke from the next table can interfere with enjoyment of food, there should be some place in the restaurant where people can enjoy cigar and pipe smoking without being hassled.

"People who wish to eat lightly should be encouraged to think of ordering an appetizer as an entree without feeling out of place."

She also enjoys the warmth and bold colors she found when she traveled in Morocco and other Mediterranean countries.

In 1987, when she began to think seriously about opening her own restaurant, she was determined that it would reflect her personal preferences.

Her long journey to her own place began in the kitchen of Boston's Maison Robert in 1971, where she worked up through the ranks, moving to the Copley Plaza Hotel in 1975. From there it was the Parker House, with her reputation as a chef growing steadily.

"My big break came in 1982 when I joined the Bostonian, a boutique European-style hotel, as executive sous chef, reporting to executive chef Jasper White," Shire recalled. "Our job was to create a first-class restaurant and one of our first steps was to introduce seasonal menus, done before in New York and Europe but new to Boston."

When White left a year later to open his own popular restaurant, Jasper's, she became the Bostonian's executive chef. "It was at the Bostonian that I learned the management skills that are necessary today," she noted.

Three years later, she was recruited to open the kitchen at the new Four Seasons Hotel in Beverly Hills. "After two years in California, I was ready to return to Boston," Shire said.

It was then that she was alerted to a new complex with space for a restaurant that was being built on Boylston Street opposite the Public Gardens in Boston's Back Bay area.

Near the theater district and such major hotels as the Westin, Copley Plaza, Marriott, Ritz Carlton, and The Four Seasons, the location was ideal.

Planning for the new restaurant began in early 1988. A *pro forma* proposal was put together to raise $1,100,000 for a 155-seat restaurant with a separate bar and lounge.

It would be almost a year before the money would be raised, architect and general contractor selected and construction begun. But six months later, in June, 1989, Biba opened.

The convincer for the investors, who knew Shire's reputation and were impressed with her plans, was her promise to present an innovative menu that would produce (at night) a $40 check average with a 32 percent food cost, and still deliver exceptional value to guests.

"Since my food costs at the hotels I worked for ranged from 38 percent to 44 percent, I had to show that a well-designed small kitchen would help in keeping control of food costs. It would also allow me to effectively train and supervise a carefully selected kitchen staff," she remembered.

Choosing the Architect

After interviewing six architects, she chose Adam Tihaney, whose credits included Hubert's in New York and the Bice restaurants in New York, Chicago, and Los Angelos.

"I loved his work, his use of woods and lighting and he responded positively to my feelings, such as wanting bold colors, lots of curves, and uncarpeted floors for a lively, bistro-like atmosphere," Shire said.

Tihaney's creation has drawn raves from reviewers and has made Biba's first-floor bar the meeting place of choice for Bostonians of all ages.

In the first-floor dining room, patterns borrowed from Turkish Kilim rugs adorn banquettes and are repeated on the ceiling to open up the area. A quarry tile floor leads to a dramatic stairway highlighted by Brazilian cherry wood. That is the route to the second-floor dining room, where the floor is the same Brazilian cherry wood highlighted by maple strips. Bold Mediterranean colors are everywhere.

She interviewed three general contractors, finally deciding on the one with the least experience in building restaurants, because "Jim Cafarelli of Cafco Construction impressed me with his professionalism and his dedication to doing a good job," Shire explained. "I also realized that this job was very important to him because it could quickly establish a reputation for him in restaurant construction.

Success from the Start

"We were successful from the day we opened our doors. It was a wonderful feeling to know that people liked what we were offering in food and atmosphere enough to return time and again. They often bring friends or recommend us to others."

Shire shares credit for the kitchen's success with her colleague of seven years, co-chef Susan Regis. Together they write the seasonal menus.

Biba's menu lists foods by type: fish, offal (organ meats), meat, starch, legumina (Roman word for vegetables), sweets, and two daily specials, one fish and one meat.

Appetizers are not listed separately, but are the first two or three items in each category.

"We want to offer enough variety at a very wide price range to attract everybody, no matter what they have to spend," Shire explained.

The menu also notes, "Cigar and pipe smoking welcome in our downstairs bar." An extensive bar-food menu is offered "to keep people at the bar when they are hungry," as Shire put it. Televisions for sports events and valet parking are plusses that have helped to keep the bar crowded from early evening to 11 P.M. or midnight most nights.

A dramatic mural curves across the far wall of the bar. Shire's only instructions to the muralist were to include a can of anchovies, a cigar smoker, a woman's bare breast, and chubby people.

"While people credit our food and decor for our continued success, the real credit goes to our key management people and our staff," Shire reflected. "Kitchen manager Uriel Pineda has done an excellent job of controlling food costs and general manager Renee LaPorte trains and supervises the front-of-the-house staff that continually receives kudos for service. Craig Gandolph put together a wine list that was named one of the 10 best by *The Wine Spectator* last year.

"I believe that it's important to treat all of our staff with respect. The kitchen was designed to be an interesting place to work in. An extra $16,000 was spent for red granite counter tops plus the mosaic floor. Art hangs on the kitchen walls and an open, non-barrier table permits congenial interaction between chefs and waiters.

"A complete garde manger kitchen nook allows for maximum productivity at mininum inconvenience to the kitchen workers turning out salads, desserts, and bar food. We've given our chefs the right tools for our menu demands: a Tandoori high-heat oven produces the hot Indian Nan bread that is part of our bread basket, and it is also used for some chicken and lamb dishes. A brick, wood-burning oven produces an excellent pizza."

Staff meals are served family style, encouraging a spirit of camaraderie that translates to happier workers functioning more efficiently.

One example of staff enthusiasm resulting in exceptional guest service is maitre 'd and dining room manager Frank King's greeting to each guest. "We're awfully glad you chose to have dinner with us at Biba," he says. A gracious "Thank you, come back again" follows guests as they leave.

Everyone a VIP

"In 1970 I was hired to manage Joe Muir's restaurant in Boca Raton, Florida," King explained. "My first night on the job people were lined up outside waiting to be admitted and as I walked to open the door, Bill Muir told me that the first two people were VIPs and to give them the best table we had.

"After seating them I asked Bill who they were. He said he didn't know, but that in his restaurant 'you treat everyone like that'. Nobody had ever said that to me in my previous 20 years in the business, but it has stuck with me ever since."

With this kind of staff support, chef/owner Shire is not about to let her end slip.

"We will continue changing our menu with the seasons, even though each change costs us $10,000 in lost revenue plus new menu printing costs," she said.

"With the introduction of a new menu we reduce by 50 percent the number of reservations we will accept for the first four days, gradually increasing to normal by the end of the first week. Sometimes it will take too long to get food to a guest as our chefs work out normal kinks. In that case we serve the guest but do not charge for that item."

"Restaurant guests want value, good service, interesting food, and a comfortable decor. I believe we'll continue to prosper as long as we remember this and never take our business for granted."

12

THE STRONG SURVIVE

"When Valerie Malfatone and I bought Edmondo's Restaurant, we made two mistakes. We didn't change the name and we continued with the same menu," said David Ghatanfard.

The first six months were a disaster, even with both partners putting in 100-hour weeks.

"People who didn't like the restaurant under the old management wouldn't come in and people who did like the previous regime looked on us as an unwelcome change in their routine," he remembered ruefully.

Backed against the wall, the partners' solution was to drop the inherited suppliers, buy a van, and search out fresh foods directly at the markets.

On his own in his role as chef, Ghatanfard researched new foods and added such delicacies as stone crab and British Guiana's "pink" shrimp ("solid meat with a bite," he said). Meat was aged for 30 days.

Instead of an advertising budget, he put the equivalent amount of money into extras for his customers. Every dinner patron received a complimentary cold antipasto before the meal. After the meal, a plate of Astor chocolate cups filled with liqueurs were placed on the table, also a gift from the house.

After four months, business improved enough to hire a cook, allowing David to work the floor. He moved from table to table, greeting, taking orders, bussing, whatever was needed. Business increased by 40 percent in three months and since then covers have increased by 15 percent every year.

Ghatanfard takes to heart a customer's comment, "The day you don't ask me how good the food is, is when I wonder if you're hiding because you're not sure about that night's dishes."

Without much street traffic, Edmondo's has to rely on repeat business and word-of-mouth.

"We have to be very, very strong to survive," Ghatanfard said.

Everybody—parking attendant, bartender, host, waiter, waitress—greets customers with a sincere "Good evening. Glad to see you. What can I do for you?"

"Seventy-five percent of customer satisfaction is the initial greeting. I repeat this at every weekly staff meeting, even though I sometimes get groans and a 'Say something new' comment," Ghatanfard related.

"We also are involved with our community. We sponsor a soccer league and help it raise money with a banquet dinner for 40 people four times a year. We support local churches and schools, the police department and the fire department."

Ghatanfard and Malfatone agree, "We can't just take. We have to give something back to our community.

Ghatanfard continued, "We never have enough customers. We cannot afford to lose anyone. The day you think you have enough business, that's the day you might as well padlock the front door."

With that philosophy, when opportunity knocks, you answer right away. At noon on a busy weekday with the back room half-full, a call to Edmondo's from the local Teamsters union asked if the restaurant could seat 60 in 30 minutes.

David said, "Give me 45 minutes." He gave every customer in the restaurant a free cocktail shrimp and offered each of them a free drink. Then he asked if he could crowd the customers from the back room into the main room. By 12:45 the back room was set up for the party of 60, many of whom had never been in the restaurant before.

A Dream Car Named Ciao's

Just when Ghatanfard was planning to indulge his long-held fantasy of owning a Mercedes 450 SEL, he and his partner were given the opportunity to take over another restaurant across the street from Edmondo's. The money that would have purchased his dream car became instead part of the down payment on the new restaurant, christened Ciao's.

He and Malfatone decided to put three food concepts—pizza, salad, and pasta—under one roof and create an ambience of casual elegance.

Everything is prepared to order in an exhibition kitchen with a wall of glass between the kitchen and dining room. The chefs and cooks are on stage and the customers are an appreciative audience.

A magnificent wood-burning brick oven produces a variety of specialty pizzas. Chefs and cooks are given license to experiment, frequently sending mini-portions of new creations out to the customers, asking for honest appraisals. Raves greeted a pizza topped with salad ingredients; 40 of them were sold the first night it was introduced.

Opened in 1987 with seating for 220, 3,000 dinners a week were being served in two years. (The previous Chinese restaurant served less than 150 a week). Thirty percent of the orders are for pizza, 25 percent for salad, and 45 percent for pasta. The average dinner check is $20. There is a lot of sharing.

An upstairs room seating 40 is being set up as a place to cap off an evening with coffee and freshly made ice cream and cake. It will have its own bar and piano player.

Ghatanfard's advice: "Don't worry about other restaurants. Pay attention to your own operation. There's always a reason for slow business, and it almost always can be traced to how well you and your people are serving your customers."

13

THE HOME THAT PEA SOUP BUILT

Build a restaurant on pea soup? Anton and Juliette Andersen did it in Buellton, California in 1924. Anton had been a chef at the Waldorf Astoria in New York, but it was Juliette's French family recipe for split pea soup that drew the crowds.

From an initial order for 10 pounds of peas (making 80 bowls), it was not long before they were buying peas by the ton. The restaurant, its front window lined with sacks of peas, was dubbed "The Home of Split Pea Soup." The Buellton location now seats 375 and a second Pea Soup Andersen's in Santa Nella, California, will seat 562. Over two million bowls of pea soup are served every year at the two restaurants.

"Eighty percent of our customers order pea soup," reported Rey Benitez, Buellton general manager and director of operations. "Ninety-five percent of our business is from tourists and almost all of them want to try the pea soup. Half of them will spend the extra 95 cents for a selection of five toppings to add to the soup."

Andersen's promotes the pea soup on the menu as part of a Traveler's Special: Danish onion/cheese bread and Danish pumpernickel bread, all you can eat of the pea soup, and a choice of beverage for $4.75. The Traveler's Special is coupled with salads or sandwiches or entrees for an additional $2.20.

"Our retail stores on the premises are a very important contributor to profits," added Benitez. "Thirty percent of the tourists spend money in our bake shop, cheese department, gourmet foods department, or our wine and gift shop."

In the wine and gift shop, sales clerk Patty Espinoza offers complimentary tastes of Danish fruit wines, usually selling one or more bottles each time.

"We have a selection of gift packs of the pea soup," Espinoza indicated. "There are four varieties, with prices ranging from $3.50 to $17.99, some including our personalized soup plates."

"We do pea soup well," Benitez said, "and we make the most out of that."

14

TAPAS GENERATED GOOD WORD OF MOUTH

A restaurant and cabaret presenting some of the biggest names in New York City entertainment, The Ballroom was tottering when Chef Felipe Rojas-Lombardi took over ownership in 1982.

"How can we be different?" was the question he posed at a meeting with general manager Jim Roberts.

"Tapas was mentioned and we became excited about expanding on the Spanish custom of restaurants offering two or three appetizer-sized portions of flavorful foods," Roberts remembered. "Felipe began intense research about tapas. A year later, five of us were spending five weeks in Spain, searching out authentic tapas recipes, learning preparation and service techniques, and selecting Spanish dishware, serving and display plates that are still used in the restaurant."

The tapas menu is the food itself, a bar-top display of 25 cold tapas selections offered at dinner with a description of each and its price on an accompanying card. Fifteen hot tapas are displayed on the back bar and the wait staff can knowledgably discuss each night's specials. A regular menu is also available at dinner. It changes seasonally with game dishes featured prominently in the fall and early winter.

The tapas concept was introduced at two big press parties. New to New York, it was embraced by the media and New Yorkers quick to respond to innovations in restaurant fare.

The Ballroom is located in a Manhattan neighborhood with little street traffic to generate walk-in business. As a destination restaurant, the favorable press write-ups brought in enough people at dinner to build a respectable trade by word of mouth, albeit slowly.

Three years later a price-fixed tapas lunch was introduced, with no limit to the number of the 15 to 20 varieties a customer could indulge in.

To jump-start the lunch business, four weekly mailings were made to American Express card holders in nearby zip codes, hitting a different 8,000 people each time.

"This was very effective in bringing a large number of new customers in very quickly," said Rojas-Lombardi. "It gave us a broad enough customer base that word-of mouth gradually built our luncheon business to 150 to 200 a week, with a check average of about $35."

"Tapas service is ideal for our adjacent cabaret," he added. "We seat 200 for entertainers such as Peggy Lee, Jack Jones, and Eartha Kitt, with cover and mininum charges sometimes reaching $45 depending on the entertainer."

"We have to serve food quickly at performance lulls, so our waiters carry trays with 12 to 14 tapas items on plates color coded for price. Customers' selections are served then and there and the waiter proceeds to the next table."

Rojas-Lombardi was born in Peru and came to the United States when he was 18. He worked five years as an assistant to food writer and consultant James Beard and was the founding chef of Dean & DeLuca, a New York-based food emporium famed for its innovative ways of merchandising fine foods.

He was also executive chef for *New York* magazine's dining room and is the executive chef of the Faculty Club at the Columbia University College of Physicians and Surgeons.

Rojas-Lombardi takes pride not only in the quality of his food but in serving only the finest spirits at his bar and in a careful selection of table and dessert wines.

"We offer a very large assortment of cognacs and Spanish brandies," he said. "Our growing variety of Madeiras, vintage ports, vintage tawny ports and some ports of the vintage, now over 20 brands, sell very well."

More than a case and a half of these wines are sold every week, at prices ranging from $16 to $62 for a four-ounce glass. Another six bottles of the house port, a 1972 Kopke, is sold each week at $8 a glass.

To Rojas-Lombardi, it's not enough to continue serving excellent food and first-class wines and spirits to an appreciative clientele.

"I'd quickly be out of business if I stopped holding my daily one-hour meetings with my kitchen and floor staff. We discuss problems from the night before as well as the new products and specials that we'll be presenting to our customers that night." he explained.

"We meet from 4:30 to 5:30 P.M. just prior to dinner. Then everybody is pumped up to greet and serve our guests with enthusiasm."

15

A STAFF THAT CARES

Joe McCully grew up in the restaurant business on New York's Long Island. In fact, the earliest McCully to own a restaurant opened Baruth's Tavern in Astoria, Long Island in 1867.

After graduating in 1969 with a degree in hotel and restaurant management from the University of Denver, Joe worked for various chains, including Specialty Restaurants, before joining his parents in opening McCully's Rooftop Seafood by the Bay in Bonita Beach, Florida in 1976.

"We held an opening party on the day after Thanksgiving, inviting everybody in the business plus the press and leading citizens," McCully remembered. "After that Florida's seasonal rush kept us very busy until summer.

"Every restaurant in Florida does well during the season. The real test is the long summer when the year-round resident has a wide choice of uncrowded places to visit, all anxious for their business."

McCully started a lavish Sunday brunch that first summer and it was an instant hit. *Gulfshore Life* magazine and other publications were soon heralding it as the best Sunday brunch in the area because of its combination of freshly prepared foods at moderate prices.

"Right from the beginning we have offered innovative menu items," he stated. "Our Rooftop Honey Mustard Dressing became so popular that we bottle it and now sell over 2,000 bottles a year at the restaurant, at local stores and through the mail."

Jean Le Boeuf, the *nom de plume* for the restaurant reviewer for the *Naples News Press*, gives the restaurant 3 1/2 stars and says, "The menu at McCully's has always been top-notch in variety and value....those who look for something different, seafood taken a step further, will really make out here."

The grouper Maison is a good example: fresh grouper with bananas and brown sugar, baked in pineapple juice, served with Bernaise and almonds.

Other summer promotions involved bringing a chef from New Orleans one year, California another year, and having them prepare their specialties for a week. The guest chefs also coached McCully's chefs, who then served the same specialties for another four weeks. A variation of this which would bypass the high cost of importing a chef is being discussed.

Saturday Cooking Classes

"We also began offering cooking classes once a month on a Saturday morning," said McCully.

For a fee of $20 per class, participants watch the restaurant's chef prepare a complete meal, which is then served to them along with appropriate wines. The fee covers all costs including food, wine, tip, tax, and copies of the recipes. Participation is limited to 40 to 50 people so that each student can comfortably take part.

"I've taken cooking courses at the Cordon Bleu in Paris and shared some of these recipes with our group of 40 at one of these classes," McCully added.

"We're very proud of our chefs and our professional service staff," he continued, "so we put cards at our entrance with the pictures and professional background of our chef Chip Yorks, assistant chef Harvey Bolan, and assistant night chef Jim Sleep."

Two of McCully's chefs are graduates of the Culinary Institute of America.

"They bring a professional attitude to work," McCully pointed out, "and they are innovative and well versed in the mechanics of cooking."

"We also give business cards to all dining room wait staffers who would like to have them," he said. "This supports their pride in their jobs. They can give these to customers who want the same service again or to friends and acquaintances, developing new business for the restaurant.

"I am fortunate that I have a staff that wants to keep on learning and is interested in creating new taste experiences for our customers."

16

NO DETAIL IS
TOO MUCH TROUBLE

The kitchen at Bern's Steak House in Tampa, Florida, is as crowded as Grand Central station at rush hour. Every week more than 1,500 dinner customers accept a waiter's invitation to take a guided tour of the kitchen. Owner Bern Laxer is the trainmaster, standing in the middle of his large kitchen simultaneously supervising waiters and cooks, greeting guests, and describing the action.

As waiter-trainees lead them through the kitchen, Bern's patrons see butchers trimming and weighing U. S. prime steaks that have been aged for five to eight weeks. They see four huge vats with groupers, snapper, pompano, and other salt water fish swimming in water monitored daily by a specialist. Order a fish and the fish man deftly nets it from a tank and prepares it to be cooked.

At another station crackers are baked to order (it takes six minutes); a slicer designed by Bern cuts round pieces of bread and cheese to top the onion soup.

"I don't want to use the same processed foods that people can get anyplace else," explained Laxer. "To give my patrons a reason to come back, I prepare almost everything from scratch."

"The quality of beef that we buy continues to improve as it's aged. We pay more for the quality and lose 75 percent of the meat's weight because of the aging and final trimming, but our customers know they are enjoying the best."

Most vegetables and many of the fruits are grown in Laxer's own organic farm located not far from the restaurant. Quaker Old Fashioned Cream Cheese is purchased in 100 case lots. Made exclusively for Bern and one other customer, the cream cheese contains no preservatives and is low in gum and salt.

Sanitation in the restaurant and the test kitchen is monitored daily by a biologist who also helps in developing new recipes and standardizing all recipe measurements.

Laxer also has a fabricating shop and designs and makes equipment exclusively for his restaurant to suit his needs. Among the ingenious devices, besides the round slicer, is one that dispenses paper towels (installed at all work stations), and another that helps age whipped cream for 24 hours, which gives it better natural body.

Freshly squeezed juices are used in every drink and only name brands of liquors are poured.

Laxer has accumulated the largest variety of wines ever assembled at any commercial restaurant and keeps many of them in a temperature-controlled working wine cellar adjacent to the kitchen. The remaining bottles are stored in six other nearby wine cellars.

On every table is a list of 300 wines that can be ordered by the glass. A per-ounce cost is next to each. The opening page of this list says,

"What are your wine choices for your dinner tonight?
You can begin with a bottle of Champagne for toasting, celebrating or just plain playing. {p. 1})
Or a glass of classic Sherry or Madeira to perk up your taste buds with a time-honored beginning. {p. 5}) And/ or...
A glass of dinner wine with your various courses—so that you might enjoy your own private banquet throughout your dinner. You have several hundred wines in the glass to choose from.) { p. 7}
Should you prefer a smaller or larger glass of wine than 5 ounces, please tell us. Should you prefer a wine not found in this list, our main wine list is right alongside of this list."

None of the bottles opened for by the glass service are connected to a nitrogen system. Because they are kept in a cool temperature-controlled room, simple re-corking keeps them fresh for at least three days. At the wine steward's discretion, wine remaining in an open bottle is blended with the house wine, creating a vin ordinaire of interesting nuances.

Diners are invited by their waiters to have coffee in privacy, upstairs at a reserved table in the new Harry Waugh Dessert Room.

This room holds 250 people in individual nooks created from the wood of wine casks. Some nooks seat two, others up to 12, Each alcove has a TV set which can be tuned into local channels or can pick up Bern's piano player on closed-circuit TV. A phone on the wall can be used to request songs from the pianist. Other buttons let guests select background music for any mood, and a nearby dance floor beckons.

An attractive 65-page menu lists desserts from Bern's bakery, after-dinner drinks, dessert wines, vintage ports, a large selection of cognacs and Armagnacs and 160 single-malt Scotches.

"If you want to be the best at anything, you can't worry about the cost. Or the trouble," Laxer tells his customers on the menu. "That's why our waiters must train for approximately a year, working at almost every station in the restaurant and on the farm—and then train for another three to twelve weeks in the dining room, before they are permitted to fully wait on you.

"And they still wear red jackets for at least one year before we feel that they are qualified to answer your every question."

He also informs his patrons (on the menu and when the check is presented), "A 12 percent service charge has been added to your check to be given to your waiter (in lieu of salary). The option of a gratuity for fine service, of course, is yours."

Over 50 percent of the people beginning the waiter training program do not finish. Those that finish, stay for a long time.

Bern and Gert Laxer have been running Bern's Steak House for over 35 years and still refuse to rest on their laurels. "The challenge for a restaurant located off the beaten track," Bern said, "is to convince tonight's customers to come back."

17

ONE OF AMERICA'S BEST CHEFS

She said, "I want a house large enough for our family to live in, for my husband's law office and room for me to open a lunch room."

But the house she and her husband fell in love with when they moved from Atlanta to Savannah, Georgia, cried out to be a restaurant, not a lunch room.

"As soon as we saw this great old mansion—it was built in 1900 as a copy of a Boston house on Beacon Hill—we knew this was our home," recalled Elizabeth Terry. "Michael, my husband, volunteered to take a year off from his law practice to get the living quarters squared away, take care of the wines and help me start up the restaurant."

That was in 1980. The Elizabeth on 37th restaurant opened in Savannah in May, 1981, and Michael Terry, still the restaurant's host and wine steward, never did go back to practicing law.

"I have always had a passion for cooking," said Elizabeth. "I made every single recipe in dozens of cook books. I watched chefs at work during trips to France and excursions to New York."

She put this interest to the test when she successfully ran a lunch counter in the back of an Atlanta wine and cheese shop from 1977 to 1980. She enjoyed restaurant work and confidently assumed the challenge of running a full-service restaurant at her new home in Savannah.

But those first years were not easy. She had no professional training and no idea of what it took to run such a restaurant. The

72

kitchen staff was new and inexperienced and some could not be depended upon to show up for work regularly.

"One night, with only one cook-helper by my side, I had to turn out 100 dinners in a three-hour period," Elizabeth said. "Today, 24 people work at the restaurant and we're more like a small manufacturer than a retailing business."

Tracking Every Item of Food

"Every single item of food that comes into the place has to be altered in some way according to my specifications. If the pork loins aren't sliced exactly right, we can lose up to 12 ounces a week, which adds up. I tell our staff that I'd rather spend that money on wages."

"Being a chef is a full-time job in itself," she continued. "The challenge of chef/ownership is remembering that the whole restaurant is yours, not just the kitchen.

"You have to be sympathetic to the problems of the front of the house, the dishwashing area, all of the equipment, and the grounds and the building. You have to be certain that your insurance is up to date, that the fish are all properly iced."

"Paying your bills on time and having a good reputation with your suppliers is especially important in a small town where your suppliers are also your customers," she emphasized.

When the restaurant first opened the menu was strongly oriented to health foods. Customers' reactions to the daily specials helped to broaden and shape the menu, which is still health driven. Produce is regularly purchased from local farmers who, because they receive a better-than-average price from the Terrys, deliver their top quality. Making it through the early years required 18 months of 18-hour days and a non-deviating dedication to serving only quality foods in a creative fashion. Chef Terry made it a point, and still does, to walk through the dining rooms a couple of times every night, talking with guests, who love meeting the chef/owner.

Word of mouth and admiring local reviews kept the business growing, but it really began to soar when the national media discovered them, beginning with this from *The New York Times* of January, 1983: "Elizabeth On 37th is widely considered the best restaurant on the Georgia Coast. Elegantly served in a turn-of-the-century home. The specialties include such local seafood dishes as Flounder Elizabeth, named for the chef, broiled in a crab, cream, and sherry sauce."

Among the many accolades that have followed were repeated recognitions of Elizabeth Terry as one of America's best chefs by James Villas writing in *Town and Country,* by Craig Claiborne of *The New York Times, Sky* Magazine (Delta Airlines), Atlanta's *Journal Constitution, Redbook* Magazine, *Lear's* magazine, *Food and Wine,* and Atlanta magazine.

While not getting the headlines that his wife gets, Michael Terry's contribution to the restaurant's success has been considerable. Managing the dining rooms and acting as host, he enjoys helping his guests to learn about and experiment with wine. On Thursday nights, guests can order any wine on the well-chosen list by the glass for 25 percent of the bottle price. Wine remaining in unfinished bottles is offered at half the glass price on Friday nights.

"We've been doing this since we opened," Michael said, "and we have many customers who look forward to these nights. We are fortunate to have a close relationship with a major importer of fine wines who selects wines not ordinarily available in Georgia. He ships them to our local distributor, earmarked to be sold to us."

Elizabeth Terry described the experience: "I learned that a restaurant is like theater. Once the curtain is up, there's no stopping the play."

18

THE FRONT OF THE HOUSE IS WHERE IT COUNTS

Oklahoma was in recession in 1984 and Vince Orza saw this as an opportunity to test his theory that there was a void in the restaurant business.

He felt that people would respond to a dinner house for families that was positioned between family-style Sizzlers and singles-style Houlihan's.

"My aim was to let a family of four eat dinner out in some style for $20 and enjoy a lunch for $12," Orza explained. "A restaurant offering good food at reasonable prices in an atmosphere not too fancy but a big step up from fast food."

The first Garfield's opened in Edmond, Oklahoma, in November, 1984. A second followed in February, 1985, testing if the success of the first was a fluke. No fluke.

By the end of 1990, 28 more Garfields had been added in Oklahoma, Texas, Kansas, Missouri, Iowa, North and South Carolina, Florida and Colorado, with no end in sight.

"The Southwest, where we have built our chain of Garfield's restaurants, has been in an extended downturn since 1984," Orza said, "and that has given us excellent real estate opportunities."

"We don't erect buildings, we take over existing facilities and renovate them, along with new space in major retail malls. All restaurants have a common thread as far as decor is concerned, but are not stamped from a cookie mold."

Managers are encouraged to individualize the dining rooms with colors complementing a standard display of posters, flags, pictures and other memorabilia. To make it fun for children, tablecloths are sheets of white paper and a cup of crayons is on every table. The crayons were also a surprise hit with teenagers and businessmen.

Wanting each Garfield's to function as a neighborhood gathering place, Orza launched a beer club. He offers over 50 beers from around the world.

Customers get a card that can be presented at any Garfield's. When 24 different beers are registered on the card, the patron's name goes on a plaque hung on the wall of the local Garfield's. He or she also gets a free prime rib dinner. When 48 beers are registered, the name is engraved on a brass strip and affixed to a bar stool or table. After all 54 beers have been sampled, a special mug with the customer's name is hung above the bar at the local branch.

Regular dinner customers who have enjoyed 10 meals receive free prime rib dinners and have their names engraved on brass plaques hung on an "Outstanding Customer Wall of Fame" in each Garfield's.

To attract new customers, Orza uses 10-second TV commercials. The spots are videotaped and deliver a compact message, highlighting one special. There's a picture of the food, a voice-over mention of the low price and the message, "You gotta go to Garfield's".

Before opening that first Garfield's, Vince Orza had been a television news anchor in Oklahoma City and a university professor of marketing for 15 years.

"All TV news programs and many feature programs are shot on videotape," he explained. "Viewers accept this as reality. We've used both film and tape, and I get the same viewer acceptance for my videotape commercials. There's no need for me to use expensive film. Coming from the TV industry, I know it's the most powerful medium for my advertising. By using 10-second commercials and videotape, I get maximum impact for my money."

"To bring customers back, we have to show them we really care that they came and we have to make them happy. If we screw up we have to let them know we're sorry and give them something to make up for it," he added. "What you don't give them is a reason to try the competition."

Orza believes strongly that restaurants don't make money in the back of the house. That's where you save money. One way to save is to utilize basic foods in a variety of dishes, offering many choices on the menu without unduly expanding the kitchen inventories.

For example, when fresh tuna was added to Garfield's menu, it was presented at least three or four ways (tuna steak sandwich, grilled tuna entree, grilled tuna salad). Money was saved because the tuna could be ordered in large quantities and spoilage was reduced, since the variety of tuna dishes enouraged more customers to order it.

Learn by Doing on the Floor

"You make money in the front of the house, and this point has been very hard to get across to my managers. At school, they have been trained to run a kitchen efficiently, but training and supervising a service staff, interacting positively with customers, and knowing when to help out on the floor can only be learned by doing," Orza said emphatically. "At one point, I had to halt expansion plans for a year while I retrained my managers on front-of-the-house selling.

"With high sales, you have room for mistakes. There is no room for error with low sales."

All waiters and waitresses present a dessert tray to every table after every meal. A sign at the entrance proclaims, "If we don't show you our dessert tray, dessert is on us." On average, 35 percent of the customers will order dessert.

When new paper tablecloths are set, whoever is setting the table must write something on the paper about food. Example: "Try our nachos!" Menus, illustrated with color photographs of food, are placed on the table along with two or three table tents.

"People read everything on the table," Orza said. "It's a prime opportunity to sell something."

Kitchen and service staffs are cross-trained, and managers learn every function from bussing to maintenance of equipment. It takes about one year, on average, to produce a well-trained manager.

"We have to develop a large pool of skilled managers to take advantage of the opportunities in the downtowns of the future—major retail malls," Orza stated. "Climate-controlled malls eliminate bad weather no-shows, attract hordes of people at times when free-standing restaurants find business slowing down—back-to-school and December, in particular."

Garfield's food costs in its mall operations are down 1 $^1/_2$ percent because people eat more finger-food items, spend less time in the restaurant, and generate faster turnover. Orza looks for main mall exposure next to leading retailers since many mall-eating decisions are spur of the moment.

He also looks for cross-merchandising opportunities such as fashion shows put on in the restaurant by mall merchants, or sports events on a large-screen TV borrowed from a mall department store. Many mall customers have never been in a Garfield's before and find that they like it. Then they visit other locations.

Orza's advice: "Be unorthodox. Be different from others, not a me-too. Don't be afraid to break the rule-book cliches."

19

BACK TO BASICS
SPARKED A TURNAROUND

Philander's was the first Oak Park, Illinois, restaurant to have a full liquor license when it opened in 1979. That and a menu of simply but professionally prepared fresh sea food, prime meats, and fresh vegetables made the restaurant immediately successful in the Chicago suburb.

After five years of success, a five-year slide set in, partly because of menu changes accompanied by higher prices and partly due to increased competition.

In January, 1989, one year after leaving the restaurant she had helped open as general manager, Carol Fiorito returned as the new owner. She chose Tim Maxwell, who had also helped open Philander's and worked for her then for nine years, as the new general manager.

A plus for them in their challenge to turn the business around was that the original kitchen staff was still on the job. This made it a simple matter to return to the original menu concept, adding a selection of innovative pastas: Linguini with Spicy Lobster, Spinach Fettucini made with fresh spinach and clams, Pasta and Broccoli sauteed in olive oil and garlic, plus Linguini with Red Clam Sauce. Menu prices were 25 percent less than the menu it replaced.

The kitchen was kept open until 10 P.M. on week nights, 11:30 P.M. on weekends, and to re-attract original customers who had drifted away, jazz groups were booked for Wednesday through Saturday nights.

"We were lucky to be able to get Joe Kelly and his band as our house jazz band on Fridays and Saturdays," Fiorito said. "He has a huge following in the Chicago area and draws a large dinner crowd who then stay for drinks. We rotate different groups on Wednesdays, Thursdays, and those weekends that Kelly's band play out of town."

Each jazz group has its own following. Fans often come back on other nights once they discover Philander's.

"We opened an outdoor cafe in the summer of 1990," reported Fiorito, "with lighter, less expensive foods. We also offer this menu in the bar area. On weekdays from 5 to 7 P.M., all food items on this menu are available at half-price plus we sell oysters for 10 cents each and shrimp for 25 cents each."

"We work very hard at giving our customers good value," added Maxwell. "We offer six different wines by the glass. Our 17 different ice cream drinks, priced at $5.50 each, are extremely popular in the summer months. Our patrons are surprised and pleased that our valet parking is complimentary."

These changes, and a lot of hard work, have paid off with business up 30 percent in the first two years of the turn-around effort.

20

ATMOSPHERE IS
NO SUBSTITUTE FOR VALUE

After six years with Victoria Station, Kevin Murray knew he wanted to open his own restaurant. Teaming up with Gil Patterson, who trained managers for Victoria Station, they visited England for a week in 1980 and returned with enough authentic artifacts to turn a large house in Huntington, Long Island, into a convincing English pub/restaurant, dubbed in British fashion The Rose and Thistle.

An English pub has to have dart teams and Rose and Thistle dart team members helped build a strong bar business while the restaurant was establishing a reputation for good food at reasonable prices.

Also helping build a bar business was a seven-day-a-week happy hour between 4 and 7 P.M. Hot and cold food were served and a wooden nickel was given with every drink. The wooden nickel could be redeemed for a free drink during happy hour on the same or any subsequent day.

"We reduced the customer's cost per drink in a unique way without emphasizing price," Murray pointed out. "Therefore we didn't create price shock when happy hour came to an end.

"But after seven years of good growth, it was obvious that to reach our full potential, we had to expand our food business."

Darting was de-emphasized to free more dining space and create a quieter atmosphere for diners. Nightly specials were introduced and regularly promoted with radio and newspaper advertising.

Mondays and Tuesdays are "Prime Rib nights," with a complete dinner, including salad bar, for $8.95.Wednesdays and Thursdays are "All You Can Eat Surf and Turf" $17.95. That menu features large cocktail shrimp, lobster halfs (from 1 1/4- to 1 1/2-pound culls), three hot shrimp dishes cooked to order, mussels, steamers, swordfish, baked clams, roast beef, turkey breast, smoked ham and soup du jour. Food costs for these specials run between 55 to 60 percent, but half the customers order from the regular menu.

On Sunday, an all-you-can-eat brunch for $12.95 is offered from 11:30 A.M. to 3 P.M. On the menu is an omelet selection, French toast, and Belgian Waffles cooked to order at the buffet, plus roast beef, turkey, ham, shrimp cocktail, pastries, croissants, and bagels.

Meal counts increased dramatically. Mondays and Tuesdays went from approximately 20 to as many as 200 customers per night; Wednesdays escalated from 60 and Thursdays from 90 to 250 nightly. The lavish, new Sunday brunch attracts 200 or more, a powerful leap from 30.

"Customers have to get value and we have to keep our menu current," said chef Tom Curry, with the restaurant from its beginning and now one of four working partners. "Every night we'll have eight or nine specials using what's in the market at a good price. Half of our specials are old-fashioned dishes like BBQ and stews, items reminescent of home cooking."

A key element in the success of Rose and Thistle has been a strong management/staff relationship with relatively low staff turnover. The relationship is built on fairness and flexibility and the recognition that both employees and the business have to make money.

The floor is closely staffed so tips are less diluted, and everybody hustles, helping each other out. When business is unexpectedly slow, some of the staff may be asked to leave early, but management also bends over backwards to accommodate individual scheduling needs.

"We have a very strong managment team that also includes Mike Barnabo, our original bartender who became a partner when Gil Patterson left about eight years ago, and Kerry Connolly, who was a marketing executive for a wine and spirits importer before joining us as a partner in mid-1988," said Murray.

"We're looking forward to opening as many as four more Rose and Thistles on Long Island, keeping them about an hour's drive from each other. We're known for good value and we have seasoned management talent eager to take on the challenge."

21

GET COMPUTER SAVVY

Carbone's restaurant was opened in 1939 by Carl Carbone's father and uncle. They were later joined by Carl and his brother Gaetano and the operation now includes third-generation of Carbones.

In 1981, the family opened Gaetano's in Hartford's hotel district, near the city's convention center and its night life.

Gaetano's is tri-partite: The Cafe seats 75 for casual dining on a non-reservation basis, the main room is a white tablecloth restaurant seating 175 and honoring reservations, and the banquet room seats 150 for private functions. Each room has its own kitchen.

For 100 to 200 "event nights" during the year, no private parties are booked. The three rooms become one large restaurant seating 350 and reservations are honored only until 5:30 P.M.

In addition to sports, concerts and theater, for Carbone's planning purposes event nights also include major trade shows, likely to draw heavy traffic from out of town.

"Most Hartford restaurants won't take reservations for event nights," said Carl Carbone, "but almost all of our customers are executives who are entertaining customers and don't want to wait on line for a table. We tell them if they are here by 5:30 we will seat them, have time to serve them well, and have them out by 7:20 P.M., in time to reach the evening's event comfortably.

"We offer the same menu and the same attentive service on event nights as on the other nights of the year. Our customers appreciate it and we are always full by 5:30. While the demands on the kitchen are tremendous, our staff puts in the extra effort needed to make certain everything runs as smoothly as possible."

Japanese Tourist Stop

The same sensitivity to customers' needs is demonstrated at the original Carbone's, still flourishing on Franklin Avenue in Hartford. It has long had an international reputation for fine dining. A recent article in a Japanese airline magazine advised readers visiting America to see the Golden Gate Bridge, the Statue of Liberty and Carbone's restaurant.

In 1985 about $1 million was spent on a complete remodeling of Carbone's. That increased seating by about 25 percent to 200 and "brought the ambience of the restaurant up to the quality of the food" in Carl Carbone's words.

"We do whatever the customer wants," Carl said. "That includes helping customers plan a menu when they want something special for a dinner party at home."

This culinary call for help is not unusual for Carbone's. It is probably a direct result of the 10-year practice of including a souvenir sheet with the menu. Titled "The Master Presents," the sheet describes the week's special entree followed by the recipe, adjusted to serve 8. Customers are encouraged to take it home.

Of course, when customers prepare the dish at home and serve it to guests, Carbone's restaurant will be the subject of conversation.

Generally full for lunch and dinner, Carbone's gross grows by 10 to 15 percent thanks to better sales and normal price increases.

"We can't rest on our laurels," Carbone warned. "We will not take our customer for granted or let ourselves get smug about our success. We are only as good as the value we deliver today and tomorrow.

"We have to stay on top of our costs so that we can maintain the profit margin that we want and still deliver excellent value to our customer."

That's why the computer has now become an integral part of the business side of the restaurant. A recently designed program coordinates all functions and events, both on- and off-premises.

This program makes it possible to create a menu, cost out every item, make adjustments to bring costs in line with the typical customer's budget, and give exact quantity recipes for any size group, minimizing waste.

The computer also punches out monthly financial analyses, long used at Carbone's for on-demand reviews of the previous month's business.

On January 1, 1989 a new approach was taken to these financial statements. All supplier costs for the previous three years were analyzed. The Carbones were surprised at the total dollar business this represented in some individual cases.

"We told our major suppliers that we were fine-tuning our own in-house costs and that we felt that they could also fine-tune their costs. We wanted them to come up with ways that they could save us five percent without any cut in quality," explained Carl.

The Carbones re-examined everything they were buying and made changes, sometimes in suppliers, sometimes in how prices were quoted, sometimes in delivery sizes.

Bonus Based On Savings

With the help of the computer, the kitchen staff was put on a twice-a-year bonus system, the amount based on food cost savings and payroll savings. Portions and waste are now under closer control.

The bar staff are also on a bonus system now, based on savings in liquor cost. Waste and over-pouring has dropped.

All employees participate in a profit-sharing retirement plan, with the yearly contribution for each employee's account based on salaries and reported tips. Employees are fully vested in the plan after three years.

Since not all employees have the same benefit needs, Carbone's is investigating the possibility of offering a cafeteria-style benefits program. Individuals could pick and choose from a menu of benefits, within a fixed dollar amount.

Each month management and staff are given sales quotas and cost targets. These goals are based on improving last year's figures. Six months after implementing these changes, profits as a percentage of sales are up three percent.

"My advice to anybody now in the restaurant business or planning to enter it is to get computer savvy. Train yourself or somebody in your management plus have a knowledgable outside consultant you can call upon as needed," Carbone said.

22

GOOD FOOD, GOOD WINE, AND SPECIAL ATTENTION

"Springfield, Missouri had been known as a 'meat and potatoes' town. But by 1988, it had a metropolitan area population of 200,000 and my brother, James, and I felt it was time to offer experimental dishes," Tom Clary remembered.

They began with Clary's Classic Catering in November, 1988. Within a few months, the catering menu had been so well accepted they opened Clary's American Grill.

"Word of mouth from our catering customers and walk-in patrons sustained us for the first three months, and we were able to afford some newspaper advertising after that," Clary reported.

"When we opened our doors we knew the clientele we needed to attract. We spelled it out on our matchbooks: 'Clary's... for those accustomed to special attention.' Thankfully, Springfield attracts many people who respond to that approach."

Fine dining with flair is how the Clary brothers and James's wife, Lisa, see the restaurant. American food influenced by cuisines of other countries results in house specialties like boneless breast of chicken grilled and topped with tomato/jalepeno relish, served with black beans and rice; marinated fresh swordfish grilled with a Korean-inspired sauce; scallops in Grand Marnier cream served over angel hair pasta, plus a variety of Indian curries as occasional specials.

Lisa's corner on the menu offers five entrees with a calorie count between 300 and 400 each, approved by the Diet Center as maintenance meals. These are not typical diet fare: boneless chicken breast sauteed with Southwestern sauce over rice with green chiles, Cioppino over angel hair pasta, fresh red snapper seared with Creole spices and poached in fish stock and lime juice with tomato and scallions, Orange roughy provencal, and chicken steamed in white wine with Pommery mustard sauce.

"We give a lot of attention to the food we serve," Clary stated, "but we give even more attention to the service. If on one visit the food is only so-so, people will still return. But if the service is sub-par, they won't come back and they'll tell their friends not to bother."

The large staff of waiters and assistant waiters are always on the floor and any waiter will help a customer at any table. Assistant waiters bus and keep water glasses and coffee cups full.

At the entrance to the restaurant, located in a small shopping center, patrons see a chalkboard listing the seven wines that will be offered by the glass that night. After being seated and ordering entrees and wines, customers are asked if they plan to have a dessert souffle, which must be prepared as they dine. People are now contemplating dessert before their appetites have been satisfied. Over half of the tables will order at least one souffle.

At dessert time, the waiter brings a selection of other desserts to the table, describes them and asks the diners to choose. Frequently, one of the brothers will approach a table with a bottle of Remy Martin Louis XIII Cognac, describing it as the centerpiece of Clary's cognac and fine liqueur collection. After extolling the virtues of the Louis XIII, Clary mentions the price: $65 for a two-ounce serving.

"Many times customers then ask for something less expensive, but we did sell six bottles in our first year and will sell more than that in 1991," Tom Clary said. "Of course, after that initial presentation, a fine cognac or Armagnac priced from $6 to $20 for a two-ounce pour seems very reasonable."

From the beginning, the Clarys honored frequent customers by putting their names on brass plaques mounted on the wall near favorite tables. Soon, other patrons were asking to add their names to the restaurant's walls. To keep it under control, the Clarys began to charge $20. Five dollars paid for the plaque, $15 was donated to the Springfield Symphony Orchestra in the customer's name.

In the first three months, 50 plaques were ordered.

23

BRANCHING OUT MAKES GOOD SENSE

"Today there are fewer luxury restaurants and fewer small operations," said Tony May, owner of La Camelia, Sandro's, and San Domenico NY, three highly regarded Italian restaurants in New York City.

"While excellence will never go out of fashion, the public today wants value. The big growth is in the middle, restaurants offering very good food at reasonable prices, along with a more casual dress code. Talent in the kitchen is also growing. Quality culinary schools are graduating many young people capable of becoming good creative chefs."

May cautions that creating a restaurant concept is fairly easy, but that maintaining it is very difficult.

"People have a tendency to relax and to taper off their efforts," he commented. "You cannot allow any slackening in execution or in standards from day one. This requires a lot of good people at the management level."

With the increasing complexity of the restaurant business, accounting costs are escalating, May pointed out. Since an accounting department, once set up, can handle three or four restaurants just as easily as handling one, it makes economic sense for restaurateurs to consider operating multiple properties.

"Versatility and diversification offer a fall-back position in case one type of operation suffers because of changes in the economy or the fickleness of customers," May said. "You will still have some properties providing income while you modify or discard the problem property."

However, owning more than one restaurant also makes it imperative to develop managers at each operation who take the same interest in its success as does the owner.

"When I open a restaurant," said May, "I select key people who can become partners. We then work closely together for two to three years to nurture a working relationship. When a formal partnership is finally established, it has an excellent chance of success."

"We serve authentic Italian cuisine using a combination of European cooking techniques and imported Italian foods," he reported. "To make up for the declining demand for wine and cocktails, we search out opportunities to purchase good wines at bargain prices so we can offer value to our customers while increasing our profit margin on each bottle."

He has also begun promoting dessert wines, offering the first glass on the house, charging for reorders. While only a few people order a second glass, dessert sales are up because customers often select a sweet to accompany the wine.

"These days, fewer of our customers stop at the bar before their meal, and I think a restaurant loses something when the bartender/customer relationship is diminished," May continued. "To counter this, we promote a special house cocktail in each of our restaurants. At San Domenico we named it for the restaurant. When customers ask for the recipe we tell them to stop at the bar and ask the bartender. At least it's an opportunity for them to get acquainted."

Looking to the future and more work for his accounting department, May is considering opening additional Sandro's restaurants, the most casual of the three he now operates.

24

ONLY RESTAURANTS WITH A VIEW

From the man who created the 94th Aero Squadron restaurants, Shanghai Red's, Castaways, Baby Doe, and now Chicago Joe's, some advice. "People want a view. I will only build a restaurant on a hilltop, on the waterfront, or at an airport with a view of a runway," Specialty Restaurants president David Tallichet said.

His first restaurants had nautical themes, three of them at waterside California locations and one atop a hill in Burbank with a breathtaking view of the valley.

It was 1973 when Tallichet built his first airport restaurant across from the Los Angeles airport.

"Couples would park and neck in that spot while watching planes take off and land. I decided to open The Proud Bird at that location, and it has been very successful although there's no dinner business in the area. Excellent lunch and banquet business pay the way," he explained.

Later, after visiting Booms restaurant at Lindbergh Field in San Diego, he conceived a theme based on Eddie Rickenbacker's famed World War I 94th Aero Squadron, which flew out of a farmhouse in Toule, France.

European-trained architect Lynn Paxton came up with the design concept that Tallichet was looking for and the first of many 94th Aero Squadron restaurants was built on private land adjacent to the airport in Denver, Colorado.

Background music from the World War I era plays continuously and authentic photos of squadron members adorn the walls.

The concept was expanded to include World War II outfits like the 56th Fighter Group, and there are now about 25 of these variously named airport restaurants operating.

With over 70 themed restaurants located from California to New York, strong management supervision is critical.

"We have had problems here," admitted Tallichet. "I believe that it's very important that in-place management have an equity interest in their operation, so almost half of ours are sub-leased to entrepreneurs. But whether we are landlords or outright owners, we have to be sure that our standards are met and profit goals attained."

There was slippage in the mid 1980s, with regional managers responsible for overseeing 10 to 12 properties too short on time to nurture under-performing properties.

By 1990, a restructuring had two senior vice presidents, Simon Vojdani and Trevor Bourne, overseeing eight field managers who each supervise a group of properties.

The first priority is to train unit managers to train hourly employees on tasks as simple as answering the phone to selling extras like dessert and beverages with meals and recommending the day's special entrees.

"We are concentrating on getting back to the basics," stated Vojdani, who is responsible for all restaurants west of the Mississippi River. "Quality service, quality food and drinks, and cleanliness.

"Basics such as waiters suggesting a specific appetizer and describing how it is prepared and what the ingredients are, instead of just saying, 'Would you like an appetizer?' We train them to take appetizer and drink orders at the same time and to try to deliver both orders to the table at the same time."

Managers stay on the floor during busy hours and evaluate two servers on every shift. Chefs monitor all food orders leaving the kitchen to ascertain that portion sizes (large) and plate presentation are standard.

"We also instruct our bar staff to acknowledge new customers immediately and take their order in less than three minutes," Vojdani went on. "And when a customer's drink is down to 1/3 full, the waiter should ask for a re-order."

A 1990 decision to prepare all juice drinks with fresh fruit has increased sales of these drinks by 20 percent. A back-bar display of fresh fruit, squeezer, and cutting board calls attention to the policy. Fruit is cut and squeezed fresh for each drink served at the bar, but prepared in quantity for table service.

"Two years ago our ratio of food sales to beverage sales was 75/25. It's now at 80/20 and our goal is to have it back at 75/25 two years from now," Vojdani added.

The six Baby Doe restaurants, named for Baby Doe Tabor, a high-living silver queen from Leadville, Colorado, who died in poverty, have disco areas that customers reach by walking through a tunnel that looks like a mine shaft.

The newest concept, Chicago Joe's, has a 26-seat bar/oyster bar offering fresh oysters, clams, and shrimp and 25 beers from around the world. An adjacent bistro serves excellent food at reasonable prices on attractively designed painted dishes.

"Our market is Middle Americans who want basic foods of good quality, priced for a good value, and a 'Disneyland-type' experience for their special-occasion dining," said Tallichet.

"I see our company growing by developing new concepts while at the same time increasing the leasing of existing operations to entrepreneurs, thus substantially decreasing the number of locations that we own and manage."

His former wife and present associate, Cecelia Tallichet, offered some final advice to restaurateurs, "Know accounting, so that every day you can put your finger on where the money is going."

25

MARKETING TACTICS THAT WORK

After 10 years of operating Wesley's restaurant, a fine dining restaurant in Virginia Beach, Virginia, James Graziadei had to bow to reality. His customers were deserting fine dining for restaurants offering less expensive food in a casual atmosphere.

When Wesley's closed at the end of 1990 to reopen under new management with a new name and format, Graziadei took over The Fountain restaurant in a semi-private clubhouse in Chesapeake, Virginia.

"We have a beautiful golf course setting, and the room to handle up to 600 people for stand-up affairs. We attract a lot of banquet, party, and meetings business," he said. "This delivers a solid year-round revenue base that takes a lot of the uncertainties out of the every-day restaurant business."

More casual than Wesley's and with a considerably lower check average, The Fountain is benfitting from marketing tactics that seem to work equally well for both types of operations.

"As I did at Wesleys, wine tastings will be presented, but with less expensive wines featured. We offer primarily wine from California, inexpensive French finds, and Australian wines, which offer very good value and people enjoy," Graziadei explained.

He'll also send out a quarterly newsletter with information on upcoming events, the same informative and easy-to-read wine column that wine consultant John Keating had written for Wesley's newsletter, plus a recipe for one of The Fountain chef's special dishes.

The wine and food editorial gives people a reason to keep the newsletter handy for quick reference, at the same time keeping his event schedule just as handy.

As at Wesleys, special *prix fixe* dinners will be offered periodically. A selction of wines will be matched with the various courses.

A successful marketing ploy that increased customer traffic at Wesleys were Executive Privilege Cards. Executive Privilege cards were issued to regular customers who visited the restaurant at least six times a year, people who entertained clients at Wesley's, and fallen-away regulars who were visiting less frequently.

The bearer of the card received a 20 percent discount on his or her party's food bill. Recipients were encouraged to lend it to friends or business associates.

A similar card offer will be made to selected customers of The Fountain but will be restricted to Executive Privilege Nights.

Frequent Diner programs have been introduced for lunch and dinner. After six meals, the seventh entree is free.

"Although The Fountain is entirely different in format and customer base from Wesley's," said Graziadei, "the need for innovative marketing strategies is the same. The key to survival in the restaurant business is the ability to adapt and the use of marketing programs to maximize revenues."

26

MURPH'S A FICTION THAT CUSTOMERS BELIEVE IN

Ed Hawkins' first job was working at an outdoor stand at New York's venerable Bear Mountain Inn in 1948. By age 17 he was running a concession in Prospect Park, Brooklyn, and by 1955 owned a diner on Manhattan's West Side. He joined the management ranks of the Brass Rail restaurant organization in 1964, transferred to Chicago to run its O'Hare Airport operation, left to run the restaurants at the Arlington and Washington Race Tracks outside of Chicago, and then returned to the New York area as a vice president for Interstate United, a foodservice conglomerate.

Then he decided it was time to open his own full service restaurant. With original partner Jim Mannion, a location was found in Franklin Square, Long Island, fronting a major highway with ample parking in an adjacent municipal parking lot.

The previous tenant had spent 11 years experimenting with different restaurant concepts without conspicuous success. With the space already vacant for several months, it was possible to negotiate an attractive 10-year lease.

After spending $150,000 on structural changes and re-decorating, the partners opened Murph's in November, 1988. A past was invented for the entirely fictional Murph. He became a likeable character who had roamed the world and on retiring, returned to Franklin Square to open a restaurant decorated with the mementos of his peripatetic life.

96

It was only natural to offer customers a taste of the fine beers that Murph had discovered as he traveled. Patrons were invited to "Taste Your Way Around The World" with over 150 of the world's best beers.

For a $10 fee (refundable after 50 different beers have been tasted), a customer receives a "passport" personalized with a photograph. As different brands of beer are ordered, visas are stamped in the passport identifying the brands and countries of origin.

DIET-A-THON REACHES OUT TO COMMUNITY

"We have to contribute to our community," Ed Hawkins said. "We can't just take. To help the homeless and the hungry, we held our first annual fund-raiser for The Interfaith Nutritional Network of Hempstead in January, 1991.

"We called on 25 men of grand stature to lose weight over an 11-week period. Each paid a $100 entrance fee, which was pooled to provide two equal prizes of $1,250 for the one who lost the most pounds and the one who lost the highest percentage of body weight. This provides the necessary incentive for an all-out effort.

"Each participant was asked to enlist sponsors who would pledge a donation for each pound lost. The weigh-out cocktail party at Murph's costs $20 per person, with all of the proceeds earmarked for the homeless. Between sponsors and party attendees we should raise about $25,000 the first year."

Murph's also contributes to blood drives conducted by local organizations. There are about six a year, and in one year Murph's gave 1,000 donors certificates for a free entree. As a result of Murph's generosity, one organization increased its turnout from 40 to 177.

"We're continuing this, of course," Hawkins promised, "and I'm sure that a year from now we'll have helped additional worthy causes. We're part of our community and feel it's important to respond to its needs."

When 50 stamps have been collected and the $10 refunded, a "Murph's World Tour of Beer" collared shirt is awarded. One hundred stamps earns the passport holder Murph's World Tour of Beers jacket.

After the first year, 160 shirts and 72 jackets had been awarded and over 900 passports were in circulation. About 20 new passports were being issued every week.

Since age is documented before passports are issued, the passport also serves as proof-of-age picture ID at Murph's.

Even though seating is limited to 99 in the dining room and bar plus 50 in a private function room, after only six months in business, weekly beer sales leveled out at upwards of 70 cases of bottled beers and 10 barrels of draught beer.

"We opened Murph's with the idea that every town is ready for a grown-up McDonalds," said Hawkins. "We keep the restaurant immaculately clean and neat and serve a grown-up variety of food—burgers, steaks, lobster, and fish."

"It's important to reach out to the community," Hawkins continued. "We let any community group use our function room, generally in conjunction with a meal, at no extra charge. When an event is being held at one of the local churches or civic organizations, we'll give them wooden nickels good for a free Irish coffee to distribute to everybody attending."

In the first two years, 10,000 wooden nickels were given out and 2,000 have been redeemed, frequently by new customers who might never have stopped in otherwise.

A "Dear Cousin" letter was sent to each of the 1,100 Murphys listed in the Nassau County telephone book, romancing Murph's background and asking them to stop by. Hawkins believes about 250 Murphys have stopped in, including one who came six months later, ammouncing he had "gotten my letter".

Although it wasn't planned, Hawkins quickly became known as Murph; he's called that now by staff as well as customers.

"If people want to call me Murph, let them," he said. "It's important to be flexible in this business.

"For instance, our first St. Patrick's Day was a blockbuster that easily could have resulted in a lot of ill will, if we hadn't thought fast on our feet.

"We advertised an 8 A.M. pre-parade brunch with the first 200 customers receiving a free Murph's shirt. When I arrived at 7:30 A.M., 40 people were waiting for the doors to open. We let them in right away and started feeding them. Three hours later, when we had to set up for a busy lunch, 640 people had been fed and another 75 were still outside, waiting."

"I couldn't serve them brunch, but a mere explanation would create ill will. So each person still on line was given a certificate for a free dinner for two that could be used any time except St. Patrick's Day. They're still talking about it."

27

DAZZLE THEM WITH DECOR AND GOOD SERVICE

"Dazzle your patrons when they walk through the door, then give them good service and reward your top selling waiters and waitresses." That's the philosophy of Bob McCain, designer and co-owner with Dave Miller of Jonathan's of Orlando, Florida, and Sebastian's in Parkersburg, West Virginia.

"People dine with their eyes—plain and drab, you missed the boat," said McCain.

A ceiling-high waterfall in Jonathan's main dining room can be viewed from adjacent dining areas. Copious stained glass, polished brass, and gleaming wood set off the plethora of plants that greet arriving guests.

While striking decor and a location near Parkersburg's biggest mall combined to put Sebastian's in the black immediately, it took a full year for Jonathan's to show a consistent profit.

Seventy percent of Jonathan's business is tourists, attracted by advertising in local guide books. The staff, understanding that tourists don't want to linger, serves lunch efficiently, but without rushing the customer. This fast service is also appreciated by local businessmen.

Gift certificates delivered through Welcome Wagon and mailings to local residents offering a free glass of wine with meals successfully brought in year-round residents.

"We have to maintain a high volume of business," said McCain. "Our food costs are high, at 42 to 44 percent, but our customers appreciate that and tell their friends. We depend on that good word-of-mouth generated by the value we put on the customer's plate."

"Since only 20 percent of our business is from beverages, profits depend on a knowledgable and dependable staff who can deliver good service while also building the check average by selling extras."

Top sales people, based on volume of sales at the end of each week, get their pick of sections and schedules for the following week. "This does not make for a freeze on schedules, with a few people locking themselves into the cream," McCain said. "Generally out of a wait staff of 65, 10 different people will be vying for the top choices over the course of a year."

"McCain and Miller really care about their employees," confirmed Bob White, night manager at Jonathan's, and his wife, Morningstar White, hostess/cashier. "At Poor Richard's, a family restaurant they ran in West Virginia before opening Sebastian's, high school students employed there who maintained a straight A average for a semester were given a $50 bonus. Employees who leave to attend out-of-area colleges are welcome back during summers and other school breaks."

When Jonathan's was opened, 15 of the staff at Sebastian's in West Virginia relocated to Orlando to help run the new restaurant.

Employees clearly feel good about management, confident that the owners are concerned and fair. But it's no free ride.

"Business comes first," McCain said. "I expect a first-class job. Then I'll be considerate on schedule flexibility and will listen to individual problems and help when possible.

"A restaurant owner has to have total commitment to his enterprise and has to know the numbers, but it is also vital to have key employees who can be trusted."

28

ADAPT QUICKLY TO CHANGE

Beginning in this business as a bar boy in Dublin, Ireland, when he was 14, the six years he sailed with the Cunard Line serving meals and tending bar on the Queen Mary, Queen Elizabeth, and the QE II were crucible years for Dan McDonnell.

"Cunard's training for waiters, captains, and bartenders is the finest in the world," stated McDonnell. "When I left them in 1970 to open and manage the Billymunk restaurant in Manhattan, I felt well prepared."

Another six years, and he entered a partnership with Nick Benvenuto to convert The Gondola on Manhattan's Third Avenue into a glistening pub called Fleet Street.

Some months and $100,000 later, they opened with a much larger bar to encourage 5 P.M. business from young executives. The lunch menu was priced midway between the neighborhood bars and the very expensive restaurants common to the area at that time.

Benvenuto was the chef and ran the kitchen. McDonnell was a full time bartender for the first year until the restaurant turned profitable enough for him to become a full time host and manager.

To forge a bond with regular customers in the early years, McDonnell engaged noted muralist Phil Corley to emblazon one of the walls in the popular upstairs dining room with a scene showing his customers, staff, and family mingling and enjoying themselves at the restaurant. Customers still like to search for the faces of old friends.

"Nostalgia is important," said McDonnell, "but we also have to adapt quickly to change."

After nearly a decade of serving several cocktails each to customers at lunch, he noticed that they were no longer ordering two or more Martinis. One cocktail, a glass of white wine, or a bottle of Perrier were the preferred orders. A new mood was setting in, and executives saw cutting down on alcohol as a way to stay fit and get ahead.

Realizing that some customers still wanted to linger at lunch and continue promising business dialogues, he began to introduce his customers to the European custom of enjoying fine port wine after a meal.

He selected a vintage port, decanted it through a muslin gauze, and decanter in hand, approached diners as they were ending their meals.

"We have an excellent vintage port that would be an splendid finish to a fine meal," he suggested.

Customers responded favorably. More than a case of vintage port is sold each month, at a price of $6.50 or better for a four-ounce glass.

With customers willing to spend more for higher quality drinks, McDonnell has increased the number of single-malt Scotch brands to five. When buying a drink for a customer who favors Scotch, he'll suggest one of these five brands. Some customers will order the more expensive single malt on their next visits.

McDonnell's second in command, Patrick Manley, added a *caveat*. "Avoid joining in the party at your own place. Smile, encourage everybody to enjoy themselves, but remember that they are here to be with their friends. It's your job to see that things run smoothly and nobody overindulges."

29

THE RESTAURANT BUSINESS IS A FANTASY

"The restaurant business is a fantasy. People coming into this business should have enough capital to pay for their mistakes," warned Peter Pratt.

Peter and Janet Pratt had their share of mistakes. They purchased a 13,000-square-foot colonial building in Yorktown Heights, New York, one hour after first seeing it. It had been an inn/restaurant, closed for about a year.

"We envisioned opening a nice little French restaurant," Peter recalled, "where we would be charming hosts to our patrons. After four months of seven-day weeks spent renovating and redecorating, I realized that I was a maintenance man and a contractor. I would also learn to be a bartender, cook, a chef and a kitchen quality-control prowler."

The contract closing for the inn was on November 9, 1965. Pratt felt it was appropriate to carry Janet over the threshold of what would also be their new home.

Across the threshold, he flipped a light switch, but got no light. Nor did the next three switches produce any light. Much later they learned that the great East Coast blackout of 1965 had begun.

At the time, Pratt remembered, "I said to Janet, can this be an omen? I was jesting, but subsequent events suggest that it might have been just that."

One week before opening they ran an ad in the local newspaper which said, "Don't Come on December 6th Because We're All Filled Up." The December 6 sellout was a private party for local dignitaries, the media and friends. On December 7, the restaurant was again packed, this time by the public.

A good start but then came the New Year's Eve debacle. "We had a French chef preparing an ambitious menu. Our waitresses were from the local village and knew nothing about French service," Pratt recounted. "Three hundred people made reservations for our two seatings and we were managing all right until another blackout hit us at 8 P.M. We were not prepared with emergency lighting, so the chef had to work by candlelight.

"Swearing and throwing pots, he soon had the waitresses all shook up and I didn't know whether to cry, run away or hide."

While some of the customers got into the spirit of things, others requested refunds and left. It was not a profitable evening.

A succession of French chefs trooped through over the next four years. When the latest one left on the day before Thanksgiving, Pratt, with no formal training, became the chef. He held the job for the next eight years.

"My wife is an excellent cook and she worked alongside me, teaching me what I needed to know. After six months of burns, bruises and long days, I was doing a pretty good job," he said.

In fact, he learned to do such a good job that some years later, when noted chef Jacques Pepin had to cancel a commitment at the last moment, Janet and Peter Pratt filled in. They became the demonstrators/chefs for a six-week Foods of All Nations extravangaza presented on the QE II's maiden Great Pacific and Orient Cruise voyage.

To serve top quality food that local people could afford and still make a profit, Pratt would drive once or twice a week to the wholesale markets in Manhattan, an hour and a half away, to buy fresh meat, poultry and vegetables. He saved 20 percent or more over local suppliers prices.

Bringing Customers Into the Woods

· The building housing Peter Pratt's Inn began as a root cellar on the Davenport family estate across from George Washington's Yorktown Heights headquarters.

In 1820, a house was built over the cellar and by the end of the Civil War, two wings had been added. It became a fashionable inn and, when a visitor inquired "Where are the girls?", Pratt learned that it had also been a brothel.

This history plus its location on a winding, hillside road 1/2 mile off a local thoroughfare gave the restaurant an aura of glamor appreciated by patrons once they found the place. But with the advertising fund depleted by the unexpectedly high renovation costs, the Pratts had to use ingenuity to generate publicity.

Pratt called on his previous experience as a broadcaster and recorded a series of 90-second food features for the local radio station. "Peter Pratt In The Kitchen" was provided to the station free; Pratt's reward was the visibility for the inn.

"We issued press releases, with pictures, for all special events that we put on plus all that were held here by customers. Wine tastings, classic car meets, weddings, etc.," Pratt said. "The restaurant has a beautiful outdoor setting which lends itself to events...and good photographs."

As long ago as 1967, Pratt introduced theatre on the back lawn with the woods as backdrop to the performances. He also produced indoor dinner theatre programs. The performing groups advertised and promoted their appearances and kept the ticket proceeds. The audiences did not spend much on food and drink, so this promotion was only marginally profitable for the restaurant, but the publicity more than made up for the cash shortfall.

"We have to communicate to people that, whatever the occasion, when they come to our restaurant they will enjoy themselves," he concluded. "The restaurant business isn't just about serving good food. We're on stage and our patrons want a good show. On many nights, the patrons are the best part of the act."

"For the first 12 years we lived comfortably but simply, because virtually all of our profits were sucked up in maintaining our 200-year-old building. Of course, we were building equity, but you can't spend equity," he said.

One major plus was that the whole family worked very hard in the restaurant and the children learned skills that serve them well today.

"Our daughter Susan learned very early that our patrons were an audience for her to practice her acting talents, first as a hostess and then as a waitress. She has been a professional actress for over 14 years, currently playing the role of Barbara Cudahy in "All My Children.""

"Our son, Loring, a very special Downs syndrome person, is excellent at, and enjoys, maintaining the bar inventory, sorting and storing linens and helping in the kitchen.

"After 13 years in business, my son Jonathan had developed into a seasoned chef under Janet's guidance, and he took over in the kitchen. I was able to phase out of the restaurant and return to broadcasting.

"But I had made a mistake originally naming the restaurant Peter Pratt's Inn. Don't ever put your name on your restaurant. Your customers will always want to see you there."

Pratt hasn't totally deserted the restaurant business. While Janet Pratt continues to own and run Pratt's Inn, Peter hosts a call-in radio show, "Food For Talk," every Saturday from 10 A.M. to 1 P.M. on 920 WHJJ in East Providence, Rhode Island.

30

COMMUNITY INVOLVEMENT PAYS OFF

"When I first opened a restaurant over 25 years ago, I thought I knew something about the business. Now I know I don't," said Garland Flaherty. "Business is continually changing and requires adaptability. I'm still working 18 hours a day, seven days a week. Fortunately, I love it."

Flaherty has 38 years experience in the restaurant business. When he and his brothers opened Flaherty's Tavern in Louisville, Kentucky, life was simpler and so was the restaurant business. For example, restaurateurs now monitor the sobriety level of customers.

"It's our responsibility to see that our guests enjoy themselves without overindulging," Flaherty stated. "In the rare case where somebody shows signs of having had too much to drink, we deter that person from driving.

"We have a stretch limousine that we will use to take people home if a cab isn't available."

Under the impetus of Anheuser-Busch, many of the city's restaurants used the TIPS (Training Intervention Procedures for Servers) program to help train employees on how to monitor customers' drinking and how to handle problem situations. Flaherty's III hostess Sue McKinny not only attended the course but became a certified TIPS instructor and conducted TIPS programs at the restaurant, until a local distributor assumed the responsibility.

Employees learn how not to serve people who appear inebriated, and how to keep customers from becoming inebriated. They also learn how to handle somebody who's had too much to drink at another establishment or at home.

"It is not enough just to refuse service. We don't want anybody driving if they're not capable, so delicate handling is required," Flaherty said.

Flaherty's limousine is used to pick up parties of four or more (at no charge) and take them home after an evening of dining and wining and dancing at the restaurant. It also becomes a VIP vehicle, meeting special guests and entertainers flying in to perform at Flaherty's III.

Entertainment is a major part of Flaherty's III draw. Ads proclaim "Live Show Entertainment seven nights a week," "Large Dance Floor, Top 40 Dance Variety Music Tuesday thru Saturday after dark." Name entertainers, like The Platters, Mickey Gilley, Billy Joe Royal, Doc Severinson, B. J. Thomas, and Mel Tillis, are booked once a month on Sunday and Monday nights. Local talent is featured the other weeks. Sundays are also singles dance nights, with a deejay from 6 to 8 P.M., a live band from 8 P.M. to midnight, plus a weekly dance contest at 10:30.

On Thursdays it's the "Fashion and Rhythm Style Show Luncheon." Parading models wearing women's fashions available from local stores alternate with dancing demonstrations by the Fred Astaire Studio Dancers. The luncheon draws from 300 to 400 people, with about 30 percent, usually retired couples and singles, remaining for an afternoon of dancing to live music. Some even stay for dinner and the evening's festivities.

Lunch is important at Flaherty's III. It attracts businessmen who enjoy socializing casually at the bar while they eat. The main bar, while large, still couldn't handle the lunch crowd, so three dry bars were set up adjacent to the main bar. The face-to-face seating arrangements generate a camaraderie that draws customers back regularly. Seven Smokeaters keep the air clean so that smokers can even enjoy pipes and cigars without affecting others.

Flaherty's ties to the Louisville community are important to his restaurant and to his personal philosophy. "Restaurateurs can't become so engrossed with their business that they forget that they're part of the community and should be contributing to the general good of that community," Flaherty said.

One of the community projects that is particularly close to his heart is an annual Christmas Party for 240 handicapped children and their families. The restaurant co-hosts the party with KOSAIR, a Shriners organization. Entertainment, food, and beverages are donated by suppliers; the restaurant donates its facilities, food preparation, and additional food, and the Shriners decorate, serve the food, and solicit enough gifts for each child to receive three.

Fighting City Hall

Flaherty also emphasized the importance of local restaurant associations, which can help fight city hall when official actions threaten business. In 1985, frustrated when the local government seemingly condoned police harassment of customers who were leaving licensed premises, he helped found the Alcohol Beverage Sales Association (ABSA). Seventy-five percent of the local licensees joined.

The group was also concerned about soaring liability insurance rates, already prohibitively expensive for many licensees. As a group, they could afford to hire a lobbyist to present their cases to authorities and this was a key factor in easing both situations.

Today the ABSA helps to promote the concept of drinking in moderation and is petitioning for stringent fines on individuals using false I.D. to purchase alcohol beverages. "The onus should be removed from the licensee who has been duped and placed on the individual, where it belongs," Flaherty stated.

Community involvement counts for a lot, but Garland Flaherty added, "Remember, good food, good drink and good customers make for success. The most important is good customers, because they attract more of the same kind. "

31

A BIT OF NEW ORLEANS ON LONG ISLAND

By the time he was 18 years old, Cy Settleman had progressed from bus boy to counterman to cook/counterman in a Brooklyn luncheonette.

Working 60-hour weeks, he also attended a culinary school, earning a degree in culinary arts in 1954, and a BS degree in hotel/restaurant management from New York University in 1963.

From 1966 to 1973, he directed the development of the Cooky's Steak Pubs from scratch to nine full-service operations. Next stop was as vice-president of operations for Ancor National Services, then operating about 100 restaurants.

Later he owned a large restaurant complex in Albany, N.Y., was director of operations for Flanagan's Big Daddy's, a large chain of discos, lounges and package stores.

Returning to Long Island, Settleman was director of the University Club at Hofstra University for five years until he and his wife, Ellie, opened Miss Ellie's Cafe in 1984 in a shopping center. Gourmet New Orleans cuisine was the theme.

"It was time for Ellie and me to create our own unique restaurant concept for Long Island. We knew that Cajun food was just starting to surge in popularity and decided to recreate New Orleans in Smithtown, Long Island," Settleman said. "With 30 years of restaurant management experience I had learned a lot about what works and what doesn't work."

"Food had to be authentic—we poured over New Orleans cookbooks and selected many recipes that we then experimented with in our test kitchen. We added unique twists to some of them, and invented some new dishes keeping the New Orleans style."

The menu offered "Stuffed Blackened Fish Cajun Style— Miss Ellie's Original Creation," jambalaya, chicken Tchapitoulas, giant shrimp "King Rex," "Miss Ellie's 30-Item Gumbo," dirty rice, hush puppies...you get the picture.

Authentic New Orleans food demanded authentic decor, and $150,000 later, when customers walked through the door of the restaurant, they felt that they had walked into The Big Easy. There was even traditional Dixieland music, at a nice "background noise level" as Settleman described it.

Seating 80 and only open for dinner, it was imperative that the serving staff sell desserts and specialty drinks.

All new employees received a staff manual welcoming them to Miss Ellie's and spelling out what was expected of them. Among the instructions: Cheerfulness, courtesy and efficiency are the key factors in bringing customers back. Selling specialty menu items is important to Miss Ellie's profits and also to the amount of money that the service staff earns.

"Don't be negative," stated the manual. "Suggestion, in a positive manner, is your most powerful means of selling.

"In order to properly describe a dish or a drink you have to know what goes into it and how it is prepared.

"The bigger the check, the bigger your tip."

Bananas Foster and The Superdome Special were dessert extravangazas that were popular and generated a lot of me-too orders when other diners saw them served. It was very important to suggest these desserts to get the ball rolling.

Adopting a successful promotion from Bourbon Street in New Orleans, Miss Ellie's offered a 24-ounce Hurricane drink in a choice of four colors. For $7.95, the customer got the drink and kept the imprinted glass.

Sixty Hurricanes a week were sold and dozens of customers ordered Sazerac cocktails, perhaps the most famous New Orleans drink. One out of four customers finished the meal with Miss Ellie's Cajun Coffee, a fresh chicory brew with French brandy, ground cloves and sugar, topped with whipped cream and a cinnamon stick.

While the sale of specialty drinks was important, the staff was trained to monitor a customer's alcohol intake and refrain from serving people who appeared to have had enough.

"This should always be handled tactfully," said Settleman. "Our staff manual instructs service personnel to inform a manager when these steps are necessary. We also stressed the importance of making certain customers are of legal age before serving alcoholic beverages."

As the staff monitored customers, so was the staff monitored with the help of an outside firm. Anonymous evaluators dined at Miss Ellie's on a regular basis. These representatives reported not only on food quality but also on the quality of service, attitudes and cleanliness.

"This is very important," explained Settleman. "When it's busy, I can't see everything. Very seldom will customers complain directly when they're unhappy. They just don't come back and they're quick to tell their friends about their unhappy experience. These reports were an early warning system and well worth their cost."

"Being successful in opening a new restaurant demands quality in food (ingredients, preparation and plate presentation), a good selection of reasonably priced wines, proper training of staff, dedicated management and keen attention to responsible consumption of alcoholic beverages," Settleman summarized.

Since this article was written, Cy and Ellie Settleman have closed Miss Ellies Cafe and retired to Florida.

32

A NEW YORK BAR
FOR LOS ANGELES

After 20 successful years writing and producing television programs, in 1986, Craig Tennis found himself unemployed.

Sounding out friends who complained because there was no bar in Los Angeles like the bars on New York's Upper East Side, he recruited 12 of them to join him in opening just such a place.

All from show business, all New Yorkers by birth or inclination, the partners realized that both the location and the name would be important in attracting the clientele they wanted, people in the entertainment business as they were.

"The name Residuals seemed a natural. Everybody in show business looks forward to the residual checks generated from reruns of ads, films, and videos," Tennis said.

One of the partners found the location. It was in a small shopping center near Universal Studios with a large segment of the entertainment industry within a two-mile radius.

"It was a double store with four walls, period," Tennis recalled, "We all pitched in to clean it up and build our dream. We economized by buying furniture and bar fixtures at auctions, leased as much equipment as possible and opened a beautiful bar on March 14, 1986, with less than $100 remaining in our bank account."

He remembered how all the partners in the Beverly Hills Saloon had brought their friends in to help launch that establishment. He asked Residuals' partners to do the same. For a couple

114

of months, the partners brought in as many as 40 to 50 people a day from the nearby studios, paying for the drinks out of their own pockets. This set a tone for the place, while generating enough volume for Residuals to be operating in the black after 45 days.

"While we saved huge equipment and labor costs by not serving food, we realized that it was important to have food for our customers to keep them from leaving when somebody in their party got hungry," Tennis recalled.

"We solved this by providing the menus of eight very fine nearby restaurants, all within walking distance. Our staff will take our customer's food order, dial the restaurant's code on our pre-programmed phone, and one of that restaurant's staff delivers the order and collects the money directly from our customer. We take no commission, all tips go to the delivering waitress or waiter, but it's a service that our customers appreciate. It keeps them here and it slows down or moderates the effect of the drinks consumed."

Tennis is the managing partner and personally involved. He busses, helps behind the bar, greets customers on a first-name basis, and introduces people to each other when he knows they have like interests. He always wears a tie and does not drink at Residuals, nor does any of the staff.

"We want our customers to know that we respect our business and that in turn engenders their respect for the bar," he explained.

"I only use premium brands in my bar well, so I don't need space to store marginally selling brands," Tennis continued. "We have a specials board at the bar to highlight good values when new premium brands are being introduced or new drinks promoted. Specialty drinks are highlighted on table tents and sell well. When we started listing specialty coffees on these table tents we increased their sales tenfold."

While business was generally good and getting better in the early days, weekend business was lagging. Sundays were slow and Saturday nights didn't pick up until after 11 P.M. Bringing in a jazz trio on Sunday nights worked so well that a blues group was then booked for Saturday nights and weekends. It took off.

The blues group still packs the place on Saturday from 9 P.M. on, but so many other clubs in the area added Sunday night jazz that Residuals switched to a Karaoke sing-along on Sunday nights. Run by Off N' Running Entertainment, two hosts lead Singing With The Hits. Sunday night business doubled.

At the same time that the decision was made to add music on weekends, one of the partners suggested giving a $5 bar credit for every residual check made out for less than $1 (one trade to a person). Hundreds of actual residual checks from $0.00 to $0.99 now adorn the walls. An exception to the under $1 rule is a $4 residual check stamped Returned For Insufficient Funds.

Further solidifying the bar's relationship with its clients, a chart tracking "Who's Doing What—And To Whom" was installed. Updated daily, it lists 75 show business regulars and where and what they're working on.

SOBERING THOUGHTS

"Even with California legislating that legal intoxication is now defined as 0.08 on a blood test, down from 0.10, our business has increased by 15 percent% in 1990 over 1989," Tennis stated. "I believe this is partly due to our emphasis on responsible drinking by our patrons. Every table has this message on a table tent:

'IF YOU DIDN'T KNOW...Effective January 1, 1990, the legal intoxication level dropped from 0.1 to 0.08. A person who weighs 160 pounds is legally drunk after only 3 drinks (cocktails, beer or wine) consumed in 90 minutes.

'MYTH: "I can drink all I want as long as I have a designated driver or I'm walking home." FACT: You can be arrested if you are intoxicated anywhere but in private, and a bar open to the public is not private.

'So please, for your protection, as well as ours, be responsible, and if you drink merely to get drunk, please stay home. But if you drink to relax and socialize, we look forward to your continued patronage and friendship. Thank you from all of us.' "

33

IT'S SHOW TIME!

Tony's Restaurant in Saint Louis, Missouri is one of the very few restaurants to receive both a five-star rating from the Mobil Restaurant Guide and five diamonds from the American Automobile Association. And yet, owner Vincent Bommarito said, "We are only as good as the last meal we served last night."

Open for dinner only, preparation for the evening's patrons begins after the last customer has been served the previous night. "We break down all of the kitchen equipment and clean it. Floors are swept and mopped and all surfaces are scrubbed spotless," Bommarito explained. "During working hours kitchen floors are swept every hour and mopped every two hours."

"We purchase the highest quality food. Our chefs are renowned for their creativity and exceptional way with classic dishes," he went on. "We keep a supply of all of our wines in temperature-controlled boxes in the kitchen, with both reds and whites always at the proper temperature.

"It's a daily part of my job to stay in touch with wine importers and distributors, keeping costs under control and my selections up to date. While many rare wines appear on my wine list, it's also important to offer a good selection of wines in the $20-per-bottle range. Many buying opportunities are represented in newly developing wine areas in Australia, Spain, and Chile. There is also a surge in the quality wines now available from Italy."

Guests arriving before their tables are ready are seated in a comfortable living room where walls are decorated with an array of plaques and award certificates. The accolades have been

117

collected over many years from consumer magazines and from prestigious restaurant industry publications such as *Restaurant Business* (Business Executive Dining Award), *Restaurants Institution magazine* (The Ivy) and *Restaurant Hospitality* magazine (The Hospitality Hall of Fame).

Each of the 70-seat dining rooms is attended by 11 tuxedo'ed captains, waiters, and assistant waiters. Original paintings hang on the walls, and there is plenty of room between tables. The atmosphere is one of unhurried gentility.

"We take nothing for granted," said Bommarito. "Every evening before opening for dinner, we have a 20-minute meeting with our service staff and review the previous night, discuss special food items for this night, discuss wine changes and restate the restaurant's philosophy—that the customer is to be greeted warmly and served graciously, whether it's a first visit or a regular. Written tests are given every two weeks."

"When the meeting is over," Bommarito continued, "I smile, straighten my tie, and announce, it's show time!"

34

WORLD FAMOUS FOOD SERVED BY WORLD FAMOUS WAITERS

"If we made you feel at home, we made a multi-million dollar mistake because you might as well stay at home. Our job is to make you feel much better than at home."

That's the message that greets every customer at The Sardine Factory Restaurant in Monterey, California, owned by Ted Balestreri and Bert Cutino.

"Bert and I had a dream in 1968. It was to create an elegant restaurant, unexcelled in offering the bounty of California's farmlands, waters, and vineyards in both classic and new dishes," Balestreri said.

"We believed people would come to a restaurant where the menu was exciting, the food superb, and the service staff attentive to their every need."

They knew what they wanted to do but they didn't have a lot of money to do it with. A condemned building amid abandoned sardine canneries on what John Steinbeck immortalized as 'Cannery Row' was all they could afford to house their dream restaurant. Fittingly they named it The Sardine Factory.

"Bert and I had worked in other Monterey restaurants so we had a following who tried us out and kept coming back with their friends," Balestreri remembered. "They had to walk up a flight of stairs—it was almost like visiting a speakeasy. People would laugh and feel that they had discovered us. We gave a lot of love to our customers and they could feel it.

119

"From opening day we offered fresh abalone served poached, grilled, or sauteed and in our own creation, Abalone Bisque, which has since become world famous," he continued. "We provided California-style food before it had a name. Artichoke Castroville is still very popular—a fresh artichoke filled with seasoned crabmeat and capers with a tomato/basil-flavored Hollandaise sauce.

"We bought a strong selection of California wines and on our first wine list we grouped American and imported wines together by the type of grape rather than the country of origin. We were proud of the quality of our California wines and presented them next to the best of France and other countries. Today we stock 140,000 bottles of wine and 85 percent of our sales are California wines."

Balestreri trained his staff to be knowledgable about wines and encouraged them to study on their own to become master sommeliers. One staff member, Fred Dame, spent three days taking the grueling exam on wine given by the Guild of Sommeliers in England and posted the highest score in the test's history.

With five sommeliers and a cellar master on the staff, there is always a knowledgable wine adviser for the guests in The Sardine Factory's five dining rooms.

This wine expertise is further put to good use at the private dinners hosted in the Wine Cellar, which seats up to 26, and where wine, food and music are blended to create the mood desired by the host.

Frequently the decor of the room will be modified to enhance the desired effect, although the room itself is memorable in its own right.

A 125-year-old-oil painting of a wine festival in Pompeii by an English master, an operating Louis XV Clock, and 16th-century chandeliers set among brick walls and wrought-iron gated wine vaults create an unforgettable setting.

"The Wine Cellar is a theater for fine dining and we can stage all aspects of the performance, from unique menus and vintage wines to music, premium cigars, cognacs and ports to make the event a memory of a lifetime," Balestreri said proudly.

The entrance to the Wine Cellar contains the name-plated wine lockers of 100 patrons who pay $120 a year to store their personal wines. An $8 corkage fee is charged for each bottle opened. This is so popular with serious wine drinkers that there are plans to add another 100 wine lockers.

But there is also a place for simplicity. The Bar Room has its own bar-and-grill menu offering soups, appetizers, pastas, and sandwiches in a casual setting. Bottled waters have opened another profit center. With California's severe water shortage, water is not served unless requested. Balestreri has added four bottled waters and instructs the staff to offer customers French, Italian, or American sparkling waters or an imported non-carbonated water.

"The key to making everything work and sending customers home with smiles on their faces is service that is above and beyond getting food to the table in a timely fashion," summed up Balestreri. "Our people attend weekly meetings where anything new is explained in detail. They wear stripes on their uniform sleeves for each year on the job and one star for every five years. We have very little turnover and most waiters have been here for at least 15 years.

"I like to introduce a waiter to his customers as 'the world-famous waiter'. When they say, famous for what?, I answer, 'impeccable service', and leave the waiter to live up to it. It always works."

35

TALK TO THE CUSTOMERS

"Restaurant owners have to talk to their customers on a regular basis," said Michael Hernandez, managing partner of Michael's Cafe, Bar & Grill in Naples, Florida.

"If the customer is not happy with the food he is served, it doesn't matter how good the owner, chef, or manager thinks it is. The only one that really counts is the customer."

Hernandez managed four restaurants in the Boston area before opening The Mad Hatter restaurant in Sanibel, Florida, in 1984. Approached in 1987 by the owners to open a restaurant in The Hisbicus Center in Naples, Florida, he accepted the challenge to succeed in a city already known for its many fine restaurants.

"We began with the idea of opening a fine dining restaurant with a casual atmosphere," he recalled. "We devised a menu that offered exciting versions of unusual foods, along with items that customers expect to find when they dine out."

Five to six specials are offered every night and 50 percent of the customers order these. Those that are particularly well received are then added to the regular menu, which is changed three to four times a year. For instance, the Fall, 1990, menu included these items that began life as specials:

Michael's Salad—Exotic lettuces tossed and served with a pistachio-crusted montrachet cheese with a raspberry vinaigrette.

Oysters from Heaven—Oysters with fresh spinach seasoned with shallots, fennel, pine nuts, garlic, a dash of Pernod, and finished with hollandaise.

Lobster Purse—Maine lobster, montrachet cheese, fresh spinach, and shiitake mushrooms wrapped in a phyllo pastry purse, served with a lobster sauce.

Chef Scott Danning brings the skills he learned in Europe to these dishes as well as to venison, rabbit, and other game meats, in what he calls American Bistro fare.

Customers May Get a Gratuity

"Our aim is to offer our customers the best product and the best service in the best atmosphere for a reasonable price," said Hernandez. "Regular customers are often given something free—a bottle of wine, a dessert—to show our gratitude for their business."

Michael's is housed in an irregularly shaped floor space on the building's second floor. Creating the comfortable atmosphere that finally evolved was a joint effort between Hernandez and his partner, Andy Smith, who also owns the Zazu restaurant on the floor below Michael's.

Carpeting solved an acoustic problem; the walls were decorated in warm colors and motifs borrowed from the Aztecs. The bar is small and to the side of the room.

"We don't market our lounge as a bar," Hernandez explained, "but as an arm of the restaurant. We offer an extensive selection of wines by the glass and premium after-dinner drinks are marketed with our food.

Advertising in local papers and on radio, plus a listing in Naples' Dining and Doing Guide, keeps the restaurant's name in front of its regular customers as well as the horde of tourists that visits Naples in season.

Managers Paul Evans and Dan Snow are on the floor along with Hernandez. They greet customers, back up waiters when needed, and generate the warmth that tells guests they are welcome. This example also energizes the service staff to be hospitable and efficient.

"This approach to the restaurant business has always worked for me," Hernandez concluded "It has been so successful here that we are soon opening a second Michael's in another part of Naples."

36

IT'S THEATER AT TABLESIDE

Phil Lehr was running a very successful restaurant in San Francisco's Hilton Hotel when his landlord closed the building for renovations "just for a short time." Three-and-a-half years later, Phil Lehr's Steakery re-opened.

"In the renovation of the Hilton Tower, our restaurant was totally gutted. When we eventually opened again, everything was new and first-class, from individual European-style Strauss crystal chandeliers for some booths to Crisa leaded crystal candle globes on every table," Lehr said.

"We always knew that our tableside preparation of food created a show-biz atmosphere that customers enjoyed, but with our reopening after such a long hiatus, we decided to really get into show business by having trained singers serve our customers and serenade them at the same time."

The first move was to hire musical director Scott McKenzie. His credentials include a master's degree in conducting from Indiana University, stints conducting for off-Broadway shows in New York, and musical arranging and studio work.

McKenzie auditions singers, most of whom have music degrees or are working towards degrees, and refers those he approves to Lehr for the final decision. Once hired, they are taught how to serve tables and paired with non-singing partners to work as teams.

Serving is the first priority, but when time is available, the singers perform. McKenzie, who also plays the piano throughout dinner, is the accompanist.

124

"We don't put on a show. We serenade the customers, frequently with their requests. When we took Valentine's Day reservations we asked if they had a special song we could sing for them," McKenzie explained. "As we work together longer, we might expand into duet singing and some ensemble work."

Although Lehr transformed the decor, he stuck with the menu that had worked so well for him in the past. The first thing people see when entering Phil Lehr's Steakery is a meat counter, a tuxedo-clad butcher, and a sign, "Welcome to Steak By The Ounce."

Since 1950, customers have been selecting the steak they want, specifying the number of ounces, and watching the butcher cut and weigh it. The mininum order is eight ounces; the average order weighs in between 12 and 14 ounces.

"Steak By The Ounce," "Pay By The Ounce," "Pay By The Gram," "Pay By The Weight," "Steakery," and the logo have all been copyrighted, trademarked, and registered by Lehr.

With 240 seats and almost every customer ordering something requiring tableside cart service, it takes two managers, Pat Sherman and Larry Ponkey. They also handle all captains' functions.

"Having specialty dishes prepared at the table adds to the magic of an evening out," Lehr said. "Many of our customers are here to celebrate something—a birthday, an anniversary, or a successful business deal. They want a touch of show biz and we give it to them."

Theatrical flair is evident in flambeed dishes, in caviar to top a baked potato at no extra charge, in coaxing diners to "fantasize a dessert and we'll make it."

The captains start by suggesting the outstanding cheese cake, then a choice of ice cream, peaches, pears, kiwi, pineapple, oranges and all of the fine liqueurs. "What would you like us to combine for a fabulous ending to your dinner?", they ask temptingly.

The favorite is a combination of ice cream or cheese cake as a base, a fruit, and a liqueur sauce prepared tableside. For the sauce, the captain melts sugar and butter and before it caramelizes, adds a squeeze of lemon and one ounce of the liqueur. As it thickens, he pours it over the dessert.

The dessert dish can be placed into a larger dish that has dry ice in it. Pouring water over the dry ice just prior to serving produces a dramatic and romantic mist.

"I first opened my restaurant in 1949, seating 45. Some things haven't changed at all—the best quality food and only prime brands of liquor in the well," said Lehr. "We have to be proud of what we sell. All of my beef is dry aged for four weeks.

"We serve a complete dinner including relish tray, and are one of the few restaurants still offering T-bone and Porterhouse steaks. But we have made some changes. We have added more fish and now give a choice of pasta or potato with our dinners. All of our dining areas are non-smoking. That brings many positive comments, even from smokers.

"A deli corner will soon be opened for the after-theater crowd with lighter fare—sandwiches, salads, and cheese selections will be available until midnight."

Lehr reflected further on his restaurant's success. "We treat our staff as people that we care about, whether it's attempting to accommodate their personal needs in scheduling or simply serving them individual meals with time to enjoy them. The way you treat your staff affects how they will treat your customers.

"In this business, change is constant. But certain things never change. You always have to be proud of what you serve and how you serve it."

37

BEWARE THE CASABLANCA SYNDROME

New York is renowned for its celebration of St. Patrick's Day. Part of the tradition is the Parade Grand Marshall's breakfast held at Ryan McFadden's restaurant in Manhattan at 7 o'clock on St. Patrick's morning. There is live TV coverage as the 250 invited celebrities and politicians leave the restaurant at 8:45, heading for services at St. Patrick's Cathedral before the start of the parade.

Ryan McFadden's serves breakfast to the public for the remainder of the morning, while a radio broadcaster works the crowd for reaction.

The TV and radio coverage give the restaurant worldwide publicity. It's not uncommon for a customer to come in months later because he or she had seen a TV clip in Europe.

Ryan McFadden's didn't set out for international celebrity. It set out to be a medium-priced restaurant serving lunch in a busy business district. It succeeded there plus it's a successful late evening gathering place for young executives.

How did owners Danny Ryan, Steve McFadden, and Louis Maguire manage to promote business from dawn to the wee hours? Promotional savvy, minds open to new technology, and old-fashioned meet-and-greet hospitality.

When, after many years of bartending and managing a restaurant, Ryan and McFadden decided to open their own place (Maguire joined them three years later), they scouted locations. A computer showroom was vacating its space on 42nd Street and Second Avenue in an area that supported both fast-food restaurants and fine, expensive restaurants.

But there was no mid-priced restaurant that would appeal both to the secretary wanting to splurge once a week and to the business executive wanting to relax with friends or entertain business associates.

For one week, Ryan and McFadden stood where the entrance to their restaurant would be and clocked the walk-by traffic between noon and 2 P.M. On the average weekday, 6,000 people walked by in those two hours. It didn't seem far-fetched that one percent could be enticed to come in for lunch. Sixty lunches a day wouldn't be a bad start. Plus the location was only a 10-minute cab ride from virtually any spot in mid-town Manhattan, with the United Nations and major hotels within walking distance.

On Thanksgiving Eve, 1979, Ryan McFadden's opened for business. Mary O'Dowd's band entertained the overflowing crowd.

Good food and drink at reasonable prices quickly built a solid weekday lunch and cocktail-hour business. By having a disc jockey begin playing at 8 P.M., a good part of the cocktail-hour crowd stayed for another hour or two. A new group began drifting in about 10 to stay until at least 1 A.M. when the deejay wrapped up.

To build the evening and late-night crowd on Saturday nights, they booked either Mary O'Dowd, who has a strong Manhattan following, or other local favorites.

Customers were entertained and the performers attracted loyal fans who might not have visited the restrurant otherwise. Advertising in local hotel magazines brought in out-of-towners.

From the beginning, the full menu was available until midnight every night and a limited menu until 3 A.M. Not only did this draw bartenders and waiters whose shifts ended earlier at other places, but local hotels whose kitchens had closed would refer their guests to Ryan McFadden's for late-night meals.

"There are nights when a large group will suddenly appear, famished after extended sightseeing, and we'll sell 80 or more hamburgers after midnight," said Ryan.

"Plus a few beers," he added.

In the summer, many Manhattan restaurantgoers head for the beaches of Long Island's high-profile Hampton communities. With friends working at or running some of the Hamptons' hot spots, Ryan McFadden's was able to showcase itself with posters at these places. They emphasized the promotion on nights when a particularly popular disc jockey was appearing. After Labor Day when the night scene shifted back to Manhattan, the deejay would be booked into Ryan McFadden's three nights a week.

These Hamptons' poster promotions went on for five years and helped considerably in recruiting new customers.

The Space Next Door

When the space next door, which had housed a health food restaurant, became vacant it was offered to Ryan, McFadden and Maguire.

If they didn't take it, somebody else might put in a restaurant that was directly competitive. They decided to upstage the potential competition by leasing the space and creating an entirely different concept. An upscale sports bar would attract a clientele not yet tapped by Ryan McFadden's and offer their regular customers a change of pace. Cafe Maguire opened in October, 1984.

Louie Maguire runs the business side of both restaurants and Danny Ryan and Steve McFadden work the floors.

One partner will cover both places days, the other will cover nights for three weeks. Then they'll switch shifts.

"This keeps us on our toes," explained Ryan, who feels it's important to the success of the business for the owner to be visible. "We generally have different regulars during the days than we do at night and with this schedule, Steve and I get to meet and talk with all of them. Since we might not have seen somebody for a few weeks, the conversations aren't as stale as if we were seeing somebody every day.

"Also, the first days on the new shift always seem to be days of discovery, spotlighting things that aren't being done the way we want them done. When you work a shift for three weeks, you're used to seeing the same employees doing the same routine and don't always pick up immediately when small things are missed."

"This is a hands-on business," Ryan said emphatically. "Owners have to be on hand at all times; absentee ownership doesn't cut it. Most weeks mean 10 hours a day, seven days for me."

A PROMOTION THAT WORKED

One Ryan McFadden promotion succeeded so well that it's now a weekly Saturday affair.

That's "5¢ Beer Night."

The partners began by trying to boost mid-week business in the early evening hours. They offered a 10-ounce glass of beer for five cents from 6 P.M. to 8 P.M. on an occasional weeknight, at first only every three or four months.

To make sure they were well positioned for the nickel beers, customers began arriving as early as 4 P.M., ordering drinks at the regular prices. By the 6 o'clock start, the bar was full and a line had formed outside.

A deejay began playing at 7:30, a half-hour before the five-cent beers would return to regular price. By 8 P.M., customers were having too good a time to think about leaving. Before the night ended, typically more than 500 customers had been served.

Bartenders enjoyed the evenings as well. Customers would pay for their nickel beers with quarters or dollar bills, leaving the change as tips.

These nights were repeated every three or four months during 1985, then monthly until mid-1988. Then the five-cent beer nights became a weekly Saturday event, with a different brand featured each week.

Ryan McFadden's doesn't open until 7 P.M. on Saturdays, but customers are lined up waiting to get in. By the 8 o'clock start for the nickel beers, the place is full. The deejay starts playing after 9 and by 10, curfew for the five-cent beers, everybody's having a good time. People passing by stop in to join the fun.

"A crowd draws a crowd," said Ryan. "And we have an even mix of men and women. Beer is no longer just for the boys."

It can lead to what Louie Maguire calls The Casablanca Syndrome.

"The Casablanca Syndrome can be very destructive to the victim's pocketbook," Maguire said. "Regular customers frequently see the owners mingling with customers, always smiling or laughing, telling jokes, talking sports—and they see Humphrey Bogart as Rick in the movie 'Casablanca.'"

"This is the way to live—eat, drink, be merry and get well paid for it is what many of them think. But reality is quite different."

In addition to the limited time he spends mixing with customers, Maguire puts in at least eight hours every day on unglamorous business details. These include seeing supplier salesmen, scheduling and managing a large staff, learning about and implementing ways to use new computer technologies, and trying to be in the mainstream of what customers want—not behind changing desires and not ahead of them.

And learning how to cook.

Maguire joined Ryan and McFadden as a partner three years after they first opened and handled the business end of the restaurant while working a full bar shift. After about two years, he gave up the bar shift to spend more time on the business side and in planning for the new restaurant.

Still, he had some free time. The partners, all former bartenders, agreed that it would be a good idea if one of them learned kitchen skills. They could better supervise kitchen costs and be more knowledgable about menu planning and equipment needs—areas where they were otherwise dependent on the chef.

Since Maguire had an interest in cooking and a little extra time, he was elected to take a six-month course at the New York Restaurant School. There were morning classes on restaurant management and afternoon classes on cooking.

The school also runs a restaurant, open to the public. Maguire worked every station in the restaurant and acquired a good understanding of cooking methods and menu preparation.

"They didn't turn me into a chef," he said, "but now I can talk to our chef intelligently and we can work together with a mutual respect for each other's ideas."

This kind of cooperation between management and chef is especially important today, with customers' food tastes in constant change.

Customers are more value and health oriented, but still want to enjoy a good hamburger—preferably without guilt.

"Everything is perception," said Maguire, "so we offer a choice—hamburgers on whole wheat or pita bread or on an English muffin. Our customers tell us they like this by ordering these variations. When they don't order something new, we'll take it off the menu and try another new idea."

The computer is now an indispensible tool. The service staff enters all food and beverage orders into the system, which routes them to the kitchen and to the service bartender.

"We can no longer think of the restaurant business as breaking even on food and making our profits on beverages," he stated. "We have to use every tool we can to reduce costs, while at the same time increasing quality. This can be done, but it requires disciplined effort by both management and staff."

The fax machine is becoming one of Ryan McFadden's profit-making tools. Local business people can fax lunch orders to be delivered to the office or to be ready to serve when they walk in the restaurant door. A possible slogan to draw the in-a-hurry lunch bunch: "42 Minutes on 42nd Street."

RUNNING A RESTAURANT IS NOT LIKE GIVING A DINNER FOR GOOD FRIENDS

For people thinking of opening their own restaurant, Danny Ryan has some good advice.

"If you enjoy entertaining small groups of friends at gourmet dinners that you have personally prepared, you have probably been told many times that you should open a restaurant.

"Restaurant reality is that instead of preparing one meal you now have to offer 26 different items, with countless variations to suit individual tastes. And it's no longer six people for dinner but perhaps a hundred or more.

"Most independent restaurants are run as partnerships. Be very careful here—you want to be certain that you and your partners can be socially compatible over a long term as well as be competent in the business area.

"You will be spending a lot of time together and this is a marriage that cannot easily be dissolved or walked away from without dire financial consequences."

38

CREATING A
TWO-TIER RESTAURANT

Martin Twist did not want to get into the restaurant business. Based in Louisville, Kentucky, his business was shipping coal and drilling for oil and gas. He leased space in the building he owned to Charleys, a very popular pub that he enjoyed visiting himself.

Then the owner of Charleys closed the restaurant. For three years Twist tried to interest somebody in re- incarnating Charleys, but he only got inquiries from firms wanting to install restaurants that he wasn't comfortable with. He kept the space vacant.

His parents had been in the restaurant business and he knew the enormous demands on his time running a restaurant would entail. When the energy recession hit Kentucky in late 1987, he had the time. He decided to recreate Charleys himself with the help of his wife, Siv.

After clearing the use of the name, their first step was to open the ground floor space, concentrating on serving a limited menu of what had previously been popular items: half-pound hamburgers, cooked to order with superior quality meat, chicken breasts marinated in olive oil and served as sandwiches or as chicken salad.

Word of mouth quickly built a business that carried the costs for the first year, while massive renovation was undertaken. First, the second floor was stripped back to the open brick walls and pine flooring that was original when the building was con-

133

structed in 1884. After nine months of hard work by the Twists and their staff, the second floor was opened, with the majestic bar that was in the original Charleys as its centerpeice.

A magnificent Steinway grand piano also commanded attention. Pianist David Barickman played New Age jazz, old standards, classical and Broadway tunes weekdays for lunch and Thursday, Friday and Saturday nights. He also performed on the nights when major attractions were filling the nearby Center For The Arts.

"I knew that musicians don't often get a chance to play on such a beautiful instrument," explained Twist, "and I thought it would help in keeping Barickman with us."

Three years later, the popular pianist is still entertaining the customers.

After the second floor opened, the first floor was closed for three months while it was also renovated.

"Siv is from Stockholm and spent some time in London before coming to Louisville," said Martin. "She suggested that we emulate a European approach of offering, in separate facilities, casual and formal dining experiences."

In March, 1990, after all remodeling was complete, they formalized this concept. "We kept the Charleys name, ambience, and casual dining menu for the ground floor and provided a separate entrance for the second floor, renaming it The Brasserie. It offered fine dining with a more formal decor," he continued.

"Brasserie waiters wear tuxedo pants and tuxedo shirts, but without a tie, to soften the formality. In 1990, business was up 50 percent from 1989. Two-thirds of our volume is at night—half from business travelers to Louisville and half from Louisville people attending downtown events.

"Right from the beginning our smoked meats have set us apart. We have our own smoker for turkey breast, pork butts, beef rounds, fresh free-range chicken and baby back ribs (the most popular). Since our smoker is outside our building, passersby frequently comment on the great smells coming from the restaurant. They make a mental note to stop in soon."

In 1990, the general manager and head chef, Herb Brodarick, was honored by the Kentuckiana Chefs Association as 1989 Chef of the Year.

PLANNING A BREW PUB WITH CHARLEYS CREAM ALE

Martin Twist had visited a large number of brew pubs (restaurants with professional brewing equipment that brew their own beers and ales) in the U.S. and England. He was impressed with the quality of the beer and its popularity with customers.

There are many brew pubs on both coasts of the U.S. but very few in mid-America," said Twist. "The last of Louisville's many breweries closed in 1980 and since Charleys has a 19th-century look, I felt a brew pub would work well.

Getting the necessary Federal license took 10 months. During that time I evaluated many systems before finding just what I wanted. I hope to install it sometime in 1991, right at the entrance to Charleys, highly visible to street traffic. We'll then add pictures of turn-of-the-century Louisville to reflect old-time values and create the feel of an 1884 pub."

But he's not waiting until then to serve Charleys ale to his customers. With Federal license in hand, he has begun producing one barrel every Sunday in Charleys kitchen. He cracks barley in a coffee grinder and steeps it like tea. After two hours, it's strained. The spent mash is discarded, hops are added, and the batch is boiled for two more hours. After the liquid passes through copper tubes coiled in ice to cool it, ale yeast is added. The brew then ferments at 65 to 75 degrees for 10 days to two weeks.

"Our customers finish off a barrel in two or three days, producing almost $2,000 in revenue for a $50 ingredient cost," Twist said proudly. "One Sunday we made a mistake. Sugar is added to produce CO_2 in the brew and we accidentally put in double the normal amount. This meant a big head which took time to settle before we could serve it, but the taste,was outstanding. The mistake became our standard, Charleys Cream Ale."

39

CLANG, CLANG WENT THE TROLLEY ... AND THE CASH REGISTER

When people enter The 1800 Club in Miami they immediately feel comfortable. The front bar is similar to the one on TV's "Cheers" and original art works abound on warm, natural mahogany walls. Tiffany lamps and hanging plants contribute to the diverting decor.

Opened as a lounge in 1955 by Bill Ader, Jr., it became a private membership club from 1973 until 1987. "The cachet of belonging to a private club restaurant was beginning to fade then," explained managing partner Bill Ader, III, "so we opened to the public."

"For the first time we had to advertise. We have always given excellent food at low prices, almost a 60 percent food cost, depending on a strong bar volume to make a profit. So we advertised 'cheap food and cheap drinks'."

New customers appreciated the ambience and the value and came back with friends.

But the out-of-the-way location was a hindrance to fast growth until the Aders realized that the Miami Arena only 10 minutes away offered a unique opportunity. The arena was notorious for massive parking headaches when events sold out.

"We have ample parking space," pointed out JoAnne Ader, Billy's wife and partner. "So we contracted with a local tour company to rent from one to three trolleys on the nights of the Miami Heat basketball team home games. The arena has 160 other events, and we optioned for other sell-out nights."

Posters in the restaurant and elsewhere plus advertising invited fans to "park your car at the restaurant, eat early or late, have some drinks and take our trolley back and forth to the arena." No parking or traffic hassles.

Drink business boomed and dinners were up by 50 percent on arena nights. That took care of fall, winter, and spring.

"But the summer season is always tough," said JoAnne. "Many Miamians head north in the summer and we don't see many visitors then. We have to develop strong promotional themes to entice the local people still here."

The 1800 Club celebrated its 35th anniversary all through the summer of 1990. Every customer with ID showing they were born in 1955, when the restaurant was launched, got 10 percent off the check. Mondays featured 55-cent burgers; Wednesdays, $3.55 chicken dinners, and other nights, $7.55 steaks. Again, good value, heavily promoted, in a friendly atmosphere paid off in customer traffic.

"I believe an important part of our success has been that there is always one of the principals here to talk to customers and make them feel as comfortable as if they were in their own living rooms," Billy Ader said.

40

GO WHERE THE CUSTOMERS ARE

"The best location to open a restaurant? The place to be is near the hotels," stated Chicago's Vic Giannotti. "On Monday through Thursday nights, they're filled with business travelers who are always looking for a good place to eat."

He believes that visitors to Chicago still search out a good steak. Even though the Giannotti name has been known for over 40 years in the Chicago area for fine Italian food, when he opened his newest restaurant near the hotels serving the O'Hare airport area, he named it Giannotti's Steak House, offering Italian Specialties.

Giannoti knows that once people taste his food, they'll come back with friends. To attract the travelers staying at nearby hotels who may be unfamiliar with his reputation or his new location, he invited every concierge from the airport area to bring a companion and be his guest at dinner.

"Concierges are proud of their knowledge of where the best restaurants are. It's important to them that the guests who go to recommended restaurants return satisfied and appreciative," he pointed out. "I want these concierges to know first-hand how fine my food is and to sample the atmosphere and entertainment that we offer. They can also see how other guests are greeted and treated."

"I've worked in 21 countries and this is the only place where nobody has ever sent food back," says veteran maitre d' Juliano Bromani. With Giannotti's almost since its opening, he had

138

as low as $12 to $15 and some for over $500. I have another hand-selected group of about 100 wines that were removed from the list when only a few of each remained in stock.

"We have three reds and three whites that our customers can choose from when they order by the glass. We serve a decent-sized nine-ounce glass of wine, charging an extra dollar over what a smaller glass might sell for."

Marcheano works hard to make it fun for his customers. A friendly hello and goodby, pictures as mementos of special occasions, and easy banter generally put patrons into a good frame of mind.

Camaraderie is evident among employees, too. With 55 employees at The Arches, only two have been on the job for less than a year. One reason is Marcheano's Christmas gift, a tradition since he bought the restaurant. Every employee receives a one-ounce gold coin.

" Gold coins are more apt to be kept for savings than the same amount in cash," he pointed out. "Everybody looks forward to receiving it and it has been that necessary nest egg at times."

Clearly, customers and staff look forward to an evening at The Arches.

42

GO ONE-ON-ONE
TO BUILD BUSINESS

In Savannah, Georgia, a city that takes pride in the preservation of its past, The Pirates' House Restaurant builds an image around its place in history.

The Herb House, now two of its 18 dining rooms, is thought to be the oldest house in the state of Georgia. It was built in 1734 as the home of the botanist of Trustees' Garden, an agricultural experiment that introduced peach trees and upland cotton to Georgia and South Carolina.

The main restaurant was opened about 1753 and first attracted sailors and pirates. The restaurant's promotion pieces play up the possibility that some of the action scenes in Robert Louis Stevenson's *Treasure Island* were set in the Pirates' House and that the legendary Captain Flint died in an upstairs room.

Much is also made of the fact that the American Museum Society lists this historic tavern as an authentic house museum.

"We advertise nationally and place attractive brochures in visiting centers of nearby states where motorists can pick them up to plan ahead," said assistant general manager Duane Morrison. "But local one-to-one contact is the strongest marketing we can do."

Morrison visits every hotel, historic inn and bed and breakfast in Savannah once every 45 days, shaking hands with front desk people and key executives.

To keep them up-to-date on the offerings of the Pirates' House when their guests ask for recommendations on where to go for dinner, the hotel and inn employees each receive a Be Our Guest card. The Be Our Guest invitation, a hand-written note on the back of Morrison's business card, is good for dinner for two. He also calls, although less frequently, on local corporate executives, and concentrates on selling fine dining at 45 South.

The 45 South facility was opened in 1984 and relocated to the Pirates' House in 1987. It has its own separate entrance. Its *a la carte* menu changes seasonally and all food served is fresh, including herbs and spices. The wine list is extensive and vintage dated.

Because Morrison's one-on-one marketing efforts for this upscale dining room target innkeepers at Savannah's better-known historic inns and bed and breakfasts plus executives of local companies, 35 percent of the business comes from out-of-town executives visiting Savannah.

Morrison also makes regular visits to the Savannah Visitors Center, where every two weeks between 3 P.M. and 5 P.M. an eight-foot-table displays Pirates' House specialties for tourists to taste. On average, 10 people will then appear for dinner at the restaurant, twice the tasting table break-even point.

Once seated, patrons are greeted with a menu highlighting one-of-a-kind offerings like Miss Edna's Seafood Bisque and The Pirates' House Original Honey Pecan Fried Chicken. Also on the menu are lighter, healthier dishes, sans cream sauces and frying oils.

"Seventy-five percent of our business is tourists and half of our business is family groups, so we find it profitable to offer a large selection of unique desserts," Morrison explained. "Dessert is a Southern tradition and we romance our guests with 'calorie-free' desserts and 'luscious pies, like mother *wishes* she could make' on a colorful dessert menu.

"Because the desserts we offer are truly unique and not available from any other restaurant in the country, we have developed a large walk-in dessert and coffee business between 2:30 and 5 in the afternoon, when the kitchen is closed for other foods, and after 9 P.M. when people who have been to a show want to finish their evening with dessert and coffee."

"Our guests are in Savannah to have fun and entering into that spirit we offer specialty drinks, many in unique mugs that are available, for an extra charge, as souvenirs," Morrison continued.

"When we opened the Treasure Island Bar and Rain Forest Lounge in 1980, we created a full-color drink menu that we present to lunch and dinner customers in the dining rooms. The color graphics helped to triple specialty drink sales in one year. Delicious Mocktails are also featured on this menu."

An attractive gift shop stocked with Savannah memorabilia is at the entrance to the restaurant. Morrison noted, "It adds to the tourists' enjoyment of their visits, while contributing to the Pirates' House bottom line."

Morrison's parting words: "Don't underestimate the importance of one-to-one marketing. Seek out your key customers, visit them, shake their hands, and ask for their business."

43

THEY BRIDGED THE GENERATION GAP

A fixture in Greenlawn, New York, since 1927, the Old Fields Inn is successful today because co-owner Frank Lepera has adapted to changing times.

"In the 1960s and '70s, we had a late dinner business from young executive couples who lingered over after-dinner drinks and listened to our piano bar singers," said Lepera.

"In the '80s this changed. Evening diners no longer lingered and the local population was aging. Not enough housing was available to new young executives to replace the normal attrition due to business relocations and retirements."

Fortunately, the Leperas had always made a practice of letting two private rooms at no charge to local civic and religious groups for meetings. This exposed a lot of people to the charm of their English-style inn and the warm hospitality to be found there. These new acquaintances increasingly scheduled small parties such as wedding rehearsal dinners, graduation, and anniversary celebrations at the Old Fields Inn.

Little did the Leperas realize in the '70s that private functions would be providing 25 percent of their business in 1990.

To compensate for the loss of late-night business and to appeal to older couples, Early Bird Dinners were introduced in 1989, with complete dinners for as little as $8.50 served seven days a week from 4:30 P.M. to 6:30 P.M. Business jumped from virtually nothing during those hours to over 100 dinners a week, with a check average of $15.

Lepera also learned to trim costs by being alert for news of auctions of equipment and supplies from restaurants, hotels, and institutional kitchens that have either gone out of business or are preparing for an extensive remodeling.

"Excellent values abound for the knowledgable buyer. I check the Sunday paper for upcoming auctions in my area of Long Island. Be alert for opportune buys," he advised.

"A big part of our success is due to the professionalism and warmth of our service staff, epitomized by Ingrid Jones, who has been with us for over 30 years," Lepera continued. "She has become a friend to many of our guests and sets an example of enthusiasm and coolness under pressure for our new hires."

The Leperas expect their six waiters and waitresses to think on their feet and handle unexpected crises without looking for management guidance.

"If something's wrong, we want it fixed immediately," says Lepera, "not 10 minutes later after discussing the problem with me. In that time, the problem gets worse and somebody wanting service has to wait. If it's broke, fix it right away."

44

COMMUNICATING WITH THE CUSTOMER

An emphasis on marketing has helped propel a single restaurant with a beer and wine license into the linchpin of a company with six restaurants and a separate catering operation.

It began when Tony Ridgway opened The Chef's Garden in Naples, Florida in 1972. By 1975, the food served at this tea-room type restaurant had been so consistently excellent that Robert Tolf, restaurant writer for *Florida Trends* and other publications, included it in his personal top ten for all of Florida.

That same year Beirne Brown joined Ridgway. A 1974 graduate of the Cornell School of Hotel Administration, he had strong beliefs in the benefits restaurants could derive from a focused marketing effort.

"When we later added a full liquor license and moved into larger space in the fashionable area of Naples and close to Port Royal, the finest residential area, it was imperative that we accurately communicate what we were," Brown recalled. "That is a casual but elegant restaurant offering fine cuisine."

"We used full-color advertisements in slick, lifestyle magazines such as *Gulfshore Life* and backed this up with radio advertising. We put no limitations on the creativity of our chefs, encouraging imaginative, American interpretations of the world's classic cuisines."

This strategy worked so well that two years later a second restaurant was opened on the floor above The Chef's Garden.

Truffles is an informal cafe serving a wide range of pasta, salads, sandwiches and innovative entrees. Moreover, Truffles has become legendary for its extraordinary desserts. A rave review in the *Naples Daily News* gave them four stars, adding "the service is exceptional and the menu is creative, with something for everyone ... Truffles offers desserts that would terrorize a calorie counter ..."

To give customers compelling reasons to visit the restaurants more frequently, a newsletter, "The Main Ingredient," was begun in 1981. It was sent to 1,800 house charge customers and 75 out-of-town "friends of the restaurant," with another 750 copies placed at the two restaurants for non-charge account customers to pick up. Today a solicitation card is offered at all restaurants for those interested in receiving the newsletter.

In that same year Cuisine Management, Inc., was founded by Ridgway and Brown to operate the two restaurants and develop expansion plans. Over the next nine years, they opened four more restaurants and developed Catering by Cuisine Management to bring their quality standards and creative cuisine into homes and businesses in southwest Florida.

As busy as he was, Brown made it a point to spend time with his customers. These informal conversations alerted him some years later to the fact that his customers did not understand the relationship among the Cuisine Management restaurants and that these restaurants were not well known outside the Naples area.

"It seemed obvious to me that somebody who loved dining at The Chef's Garden would be willing to try Villa Pescatore or Plum's Cafe in North Naples if they knew it was under the same ownership," Brown said. "So we hired a full-time marketing agency to heighten awareness in the public's mind of the restaurants as individual entities and as part of the Cuisine Management family. I also reclaimed the editing and publishing responsibilities for our newsletter. The marketing agency developed direct mail pieces and a 10th Anniversary Celebration for The Chef's Garden that was so successful it was repeated two years later for the 10th anniversary of Truffles."

Customers were given a sized-down replica of the front page of the Naples newspaper for the day each restaurant opened, with pictures and stories of the restaurant's 10-year history on the flip side.

Focus Groups With Customers

Kim Bratton, hired in October, 1989 as marketing director, came up with the idea of picking 10 to 12 good customers of each restaurant for a focus group. They were invited to a luncheon with the managers and asked for their likes and dislikes. To keep the atmosphere relaxed, the owners were not present.

Management meetings followed, both collective and one-on-one, to assess what was heard and to plan action. The focus groups are now semi-annual exercises for each restaurant, with different groups of customers invited each time.

A management consultant, Jan Kantor, was hired to increase communications between staff and management, management and management, everybody and the owners. A new full-time director-of-service position was also established to supervise special projects and staff training, co-ordinating with consultant Kantor, who serves about five to eight hours a week.

"Training is very important," said Brown. "All staff took nine full days of training before we opened our newest restaurant, Bayside."

Beginning at 9 A.M. and lasting until 3:15 P. M., the training sessions include almost daily attention to the use of computers, wine education, menu education, service and floor procedures, plus classes on role playing, proper grooming and proper attire. Tests were given on the seventh day and reviewed on the ninth day.

"We believe that the restaurant business can be pictured as an inverted pyramid," Brown summed up. "The customers are at the top of this upside-down pyramid, supported by descending layers of staff, mid-management, top management, and owners. Everybody in the organization has a responsibility to the customer and all management has to be supportive of the staff's efforts."

45

BARTER FOR ADVERTISING

Beginning as a 12-year-old bus boy in 1949, Chicago restaurateur Art Greco opened his first restaurant, Greco's, in 1971. Excellent Italian food was served fiesta style: Customers were seated at banquet-style tables, given extra- large plates, and encouraged to share foods with others at the same table. A clientele who felt comfortable in table hopping and talking across the room quickly developed and grew as the people having fun brought in relatives and friends, some of whom also became regulars.

After a year and a half, Greco expanded the rear dining room and installed a piano in the front room with the bar, to entertain customers late into the night.

Before the expansion, the 65-seat restaurant was grossing $1 million a year. After expanding to 200 seats, which were filled only on Friday and Saturday nights, business increased to a million and a half a year.

Greco soon opened his first Artie G's in the Balos Heights suburb of Chicago. It was a combination night club and restaurant serving Neapolitan Italian food for lunch and dinner. Successful there for five years, his landlord declined to renew the lease. Now what?

Greco decided to join the big time, reopening in downtown Chicago—and learned an expensive lesson. Everybody in the local media descended on the "new kid on the block" with reasons why their publications were necessary vehicles for advertising.

150

46

A NETWORK OF FRIENDS IS A NETWORK OF CUSTOMERS

"If you want to be in business five years from now, you have to get involved with your customers," said Eamonn Doran, whose popular Eamonn Doran's restaurant on New York's East Side was opened in 1977.

"My basic premise is that I'm in business to give my customers what they want—food that is consistently good, a kitchen that stays open as long as the restaurant is open (to 4 A.M. every night), pints of the world's best beers, and a staff that understands that the word 'no' is taboo.

"If a customer asks for something that we don't have, I want somebody to try to find it at one of the delis, supermarkets or fruit stands that stay open here 24 hours a day. We might be the first stop for people coming to New York from other parts of the country or the world, and I want to accommodate them."

Doran and his staff spend time introducing one person to another in the bar area. As customers get to know each other, the bar becomes a base for socializing. Another lure for old and new patrons is videotapes of international championship rugby and soccer games. They're available at Doran's less than 24 hours after the games have been played in Europe. In the audience—and at the bar—are UN staffers and waiters from nearby French and Italian restaurants who visit between shifts. (The videotapes are played on request, but without sound so they don't interfere with conversation.)

Group trips to rugby games in Ireland as well as in the New York area are regular events. Impromptu theater parties are organized when customers or friends are involved in a theatrical production. The restaurant's vestibule has become a notice board, with space donated to promote arts and entertainment events, many of them Irish.

"The first Christmas that we were open, in 1977, was eventful for us in two ways," Doran remembered. "One of our customers, who is in the communications business, held a waifs-and-strays Christmas day dinner at our restaurant. He invited his journalist friends and acquaintances from other countries who were without family or friends at Christmas.

"This became an annual event. Many of these guests are regulars when they are in New York and have written about our restaurant in their home publications. Almost every week somebody comes in and mentions such a write-up as the reason they stopped by."

The other momentous event began as a simple raffle to raise money for Christmas presents for children at the New York Foundling Hospital.

"I believe I have to share any good fortune I have with others less fortunate," said Doran. "I asked my brother Dermott—he's a Catholic priest in the Holy Ghost Order who runs a relief agency for third-world countries—to recommend a charity. That was the New York Foundling Hospital.

"That year we were able to donate six quality stereo systems. In the next 13 years, we raised over $250,000 through the generosity of the customers who attended our annual golf outings. We added a formal Red Tie Valentine's Dinner in 1991 expecting to raise double the annual sum."

"I can't point to specific business that we've attracted because of these efforts," he reflected, "but I feel happy, I've made many friends, and my business has been good no matter what has been happening to the general economy."

One substantial reason for the good business is that Doran doesn't believe in waiting for people to walk through the door so he can work his magic on them.

"People change jobs, firms relocate, people die—unless new customers are regularly attracted you can be out of business and wondering why," he said.

"I'm constantly being invited to social, business, or cultural affairs, sometimes in other parts of the country, and I attend as many as I can. This has given me exposure to thousands of people who have never been in my restaurant. Many of them do later visit."

The flip side of this is that when he travels, he is not at his restaurant to greet and mingle with the customers. That is where the "club" atmosphere he has established pays off. Customers socialize even when he is not present. Also important is the well-trained and loyal staff who interact with customers with much the same cordiality as he does.

Many customers have become part of his extended family and he celebrates with them at weddings and offers sympathy when that is appropriate.

In 1986, for instance, six businessmen from Ireland sailed a Currach-class boat to New York to participate in Fourth of July festivities. They mentioned over dinner at Doran's that they needed money to ship the boat back to Ireland. Loading the boat with champagne, smoked salmon and brown bread, Doran convinced 25 of his customers to join him for a sail among the hundreds of ships in New York Harbor that were also participating in the festivities. A hat was later passed raising more than enough money to return the boat to Ireland.

Four years later, Paddy Barry, one of the group, called to make a dinner reservation for 12. Invited to New York to receive a prestigious award from the New York Yacht Club, the 12 were planning on dinner at Doran's the night before the event. Barry also mentioned that he and his friends had put out the word about Eamonn's to their New-York bound Irish acquaintances.

Other Irish visiting Doran's strike up friendships that continue after they return to Ireland. One of Doran's bartenders, Sean Smith, visited Ireland for the first time in seven years and 150 Doran acquaintances turned out for a welcoming party.

Important to the conviviality is consistently excellent food that is also offbeat: Gaelic steak, Doran's chicken (which he prepared on the "Live With Regis and Kathie Lee" TV show on St. Patrick's Day in 1990), four Irish pies—Shepherd's, steak and kidney, fish, and chicken, plus a 10-ounce hamburger served on an eight-ounce roll, and an outstanding Irish sherry trifle.

At the bar, Eamonn Doran's has earned a reputation for serving a memorable Irish coffee, a large selection of American and international beers, many on tap, and the best Guinness Stout in Manhattan.

How to Draw Stout

There is a knack to drawing a good pint of Guinness Stout. Bartender Liam Conaty says it helps to sell a lot of it so that the brew is always fresh, but clean pipes are essential and the serving temperature should be 45 degrees.

"Don't hurry the pour," he instructed. "Always use a dry glass and pause after filling it two-thirds full. Let it settle two or three minutes before topping it off.

"When it comes to Irish coffee, pour a full 1 1/2 ounces of Jameson's Irish whiskey into the coffee, add one teaspoon of brown sugar and then top it with heavy cream that you put in the blender for 15 seconds just before adding it."

In 1988, testing expansion potential, Doran allowed a friend of 25 years, Christian Dubreuil, to open another Eamonn Doran's in the Penta Hotel, across from Madison Square Garden on New York's West Side.

Success at the Penta encouraged Doran, and his wife Clare opened Eamonn Doran's Marmalade Park restaurant in New York's East Gate Tower Hotel in March, 1991. Additional expansion around the country, possibly on a joint venture or franchise basis, is under consideration.

"Restaurateurs today have to be alert to what our customers tell us," Doran mused. "As successful as my original place has been, I have plans in mind for major changes. I want to expand from a dining room seating 60 in 3,000 feet to 15,000 square feet on two or three floors and offer separate environments for business lunches, sports activities, private parties, and live entertainment."

"We'll keep our traditional menu specialties and add some new items and we'll open for breakfast, which is becoming very popular for business meetings."

Part III

EXPERT ADVICE

47

RESTAURANT ASSOCIATIONS
United We Profit, Divided We Are Vulnerable

Local, state, or national government legislators can put many restaurants out of business by enacting some or all of the restrictive legislation that special interest groups propose.

"One suggestion continually coming up is that restaurants provide ingredient and nutritional information on menus similar to labels on packaged foods," explained William Fisher, executive vice president of the National Restaurant Association, based in Washington, D.C. "This sounds fair until you realize that this virtually eliminates creativity and flexibility by the chef. He could no longer improvise on items on the menu and would function as a cookie cutter.

"Restaurants offering daily specials based on that morning's market availability would have a horrendous, if not impossible, clerical burden imposed on them."

Another danger zone is deductibility of meals. As it looks for new revenue sources every year, Congress, which reduced the tax deductibility of meals as a business expenses to 80 percent in 1986, periodically considers further reducing deductibility to 50 percent.

"It would be fair to say that business firms already cutting advertising and promotion costs, which are fully deductible, would react to such a move by sharply cutting back their restaurant business meals," Fisher commented.

"Another issue that keeps surfacing is mandated benefits for employees," he continued. "This would be very expensive and an impossible burden for many independent restaurateurs. This is an issue that should be handled according to local conditions."

Restaurant operators are exposed to multiple government restrictions in the areas of health and safety at local, state and federal levels. State regulations often match or exceed federal regulations in strictness.

"The National Restaurant Association is the restaurant operator's voice to Congress," said Fisher. "We meet with key Congressmen regularly to present our industry's side on the myriad restrictive proposals that arise."

"But this is only one facet of what we do. First and foremost is service to our individual members - the restaurateurs of America," he continued. "We sponsor 200 seminars a year around the country on purchasing, dining room management, and food and beverage management among other subjects.

"We have videotapes available for staff training, including alcohol beverage server awareness training programs. Our members receive our various periodicals, including the monthly *Restaurants USA*, can participate in a variety of group insurance plans for members and employees, and can call our information and library service for anything from industry trends to recipes."

"The strength of the restaurant industry, and of the individual restaurant depends on the strength of the local, state, and national restaurant associations and the links among them," Fisher emphasized. "Every restaurateur should be an active member of the local association. There, an individual voice can be heard and local problems can be confronted with strength."

"You should also participate in your state association activities and belong to the National Restaurant Association. That assures access to all the help we have to offer plus it strengthens our hand in dealing with the government."

How to Join

For information about membership in the National Restaurant Association and on contacting state and local associations, call (800) 424-5156 toll-free and ask for membership information. In 20 states, a single fee pays for membership in both the state and national restaurant associations.

48

GOOD RESTAURANTS MAKE PEOPLE HAPPY

"Restaurants don't sell food and beverages for a profit," Cornell University's Tom Kelly pointed out. "They sell an experience. Successful restaurateurs make people happy, they don't just serve a steak."

This isn't ivory tower talk that sounds good in the classroom but won't cut it in the real world. Although he's now an associate professor in the Cornell University School of Hotel Administration, Kelly worked at every restaurant job possible for nine years then spent another five years as partner/general manager of an Ithaca-area restaurant/night club.

During those years he also taught restaurant management at Cortland Community College. He finally opted for the academic path and returned to Cornell, his alma mater.

He continues to consult for restaurants and institutions all over the world, which also helps him keep abreast of industry advances.

"I never let consulting assignments interfere with my academic work load," Kelly said. "Actually, the research and analysis that I've undertaken for private clients often shows up as classroom material, disguised, of course, so as not to betray confidences."

Consulting generally falls into two categories: One-time efforts to help jump-start new ventures or to fine-tune existing operations or on-going, usually monthly consultations.

160

49

SINGLE MALT SCOTCHES DRAW A CROWD

Although Keens Chop House had been a New York City landmark for 100 years, its temporary closing and later reopening as Keens Restaurant caused general manager Phil Nugent to look for the unique niche that would set Keens bar apart from every other bar in the city.

"Come up with a promotional theme for our bar that nobody else has," he challenged bar manager Dan Beck.

At that time, Keens lunch customers were executives from nearby businesses, and at night businessmen from around the country who were in town for conventions or to call on Manhattan customers. They enjoyed cocktails and imported beers, so Beck felt they would be interested in cognac and Scotch—categories he decided to bone up on.

At a downtown New York restaurant noted for offering seven different single malt Scotches, Beck found the theme he was looking for.

"The intensity and range of the flavors and the depth of character of the brands just blew me away," he remembered.

"That was it. I began purchasing two or three bottles of every brand of single malt Scotch available from New York distributors. I read everything available about the category, which wasn't very much. I also questioned suppliers constantly, searching for additional knowledge about each brand."

With 17 different brands on the back bar, now what? Offering taste samples to Scotch drinkers was a start. Almost ten percent enjoyed it enough to subsequently order a single malt, experimenting with the different brands much as wine drinkers enjoy comparing one Cabernet Sauvignon to another.

After three months, 150 customers had expressed interest in attending a more formal tasting of single malts where they could also learn something about this category of spirits.

"I had no examples of formal whiskey tastings to follow," Beck said, "so I had to devise my own approach."

A Piper Calls

The agenda: A call to the tasting tables by a bagpiper in full Scottish regalia, an introductory talk about single malt Scotchs by an industry representative, and a talk-through of the tasting of four single malt brands, with crackers and water at each place to clear palates.

Each whisky to be tasted was cut with an equal amount of water, which released its flavors, while an uncut serving of each was available for guests to "nose". (Beck even devised a nosing technique: Exhale, put nose into glass, breathe in slowly through the mouth.)

Tasters were encouraged to share their reactions with the group. A camaraderie was quickly established that made for easy interplay when everybody adjourned to an open bar for the second hour to sample other single malts in the Keens' collection. Accompanying the open bar were an assortment of Scottish cheeses, Scotch eggs, and meat pies.

Beck hosted 25 tastings in seven years at Keens. After the first four, he realized he knew more about the category than industry representatives, had accumulated interesting anecdotal and historical data, and had a good feel for what his customers wanted to know about single malts.

Coupled with the fast-developing personal tasting abilities that allowed him to lead his guests through the nuances of each whisky, he decided it was time to assume the mantle of educator and bon vivant at these affairs.

At the same time, official bagpiper Roger Parson developed an interest in the subject and after considerable study, he joined Beck in forming Spirited Tastings, Inc. in 1987.

The first bookings for Spirited Tastings were at New York area country clubs, generally as part of a membership gala. After only two years, requests for these tastings were coming in from all parts of the country.

Beck and Parson frequently work with interested restaurateurs in training management and staff to plan and promote similar events. A booklet, "Developing a successful ongoing single malt Scotch program," is available at no charge from Spirited Tastings, Inc., 123 Bergen Avenue, Ridgefield Park, NJ 07660. Telephone: (201) 440-9299.

50

YOU ONLY MAKE A
FIRST IMPRESSION ONCE

"What's the first impression you make on your customers when you seat them?" asked Ray Hagan, whose New York marketing agency has represented many of the finest manufacturers of tabletop supplies for over 30 years.

"Not the quality of your food. Not the excellence of your service. The first thing your customers see is your tabletop. Generally, it is boring at best."

Broaden your thinking, he suggested. "Don't limit yourself to selections available from the average restaurant equipment dealer. Look for upscale, interesting dealers. Many of them congregate in the design buildings found in major urban centers. Buildings like 225 Fifth Avenue in New York, one of Hagan's accounts, are filled with showrooms of distributors offering fine china and flatware."

"Thinner is stronger than thicker," Hagan advised. "Porcelain china is much stronger and more chip-resistant than earthenware and is certainly more beautiful. Lead crystal is as strong as tempered glass and can be equally dishwasher safe."

Hagan believes that by greeting customers with a striking tabletop, you are setting the stage for the full appreciation of the food and drinks you will serve.

"You expect more from and will pay more for a show at a Broadway theater than for the same show with the same cast performing at the local theater in the round. Create anticipation for your customers and then fulfill that anticipation with outstanding food and drink," he said. "Isn't that why you are, or want to be, in the restaurant business?"

"If you plan on using service plates, you don't have to limit your horizons to porcelain," Hagan continued. "Look at stainless steel, brass, silverplate, Wilton Armetale, and Italian hand-painted ceramic plates."

"Have celebratory service plates to use for birthdays and anniversarys. Personalize them if the customer agrees, and make an extra profit by selling them as souvenirs to members of the party."

"Have a full service of Christmas tableware and accessories. Use this for the Christmas parties that you book for the three weeks prior to Christmas and for Christmas Day."

Hagan warns against buying flatware so light that it can be bent by hand. Customers flinch and wonder where else you might be skimping. He also cautions about using silver-plated flatware.

"If you want silver, buy sterling. Silverplate won't stand up well to constant commercial dishwashing. If you insist on silverplate, some European flatware has bigger and bolder sizes which make for an impressive presentation.

"If you pride yourself on your wines and cocktails, serve them in crystal. Use the recommended sizes for red Bordeaux and Burgundy and white wines, always flute glasses for champagne, not the saucer shapes. A glass made of thin crystal stemware with a classic flaring shape for Martinis and Manhattans will have your customers enjoying their drinks before they even take that first sip."

Potash glassware that imitates full lead crystal won't fool knowledgable customers, Hagan advised. The latest lead crystal manufacturing techniques allow close duplication of expensive mouth-blown crystal stemware at reasonable prices.

"Buy a new look for your tabletops every month by selecting figurines, vases, lamps, uniquely shaped boxes, or seasonal items. They are all on display at gift and decorative display showrooms in the design buildings," Hagan suggested. "You might even have a surprise profit center if enough customers want to purchase these items from you."

51

A PR PROFESSIONAL IS A BIG PLUS

Any restaurant with facilities for private functions will benefit from the advice of a skilled public relations professional who also has experience in planning meetings and parties. So said Sharon Malone, speaking from her experience as president of Main Event International, a firm that offered public relations and party planning services to restaurateurs. Here's her advice on how to work with PR consultants.

Using a public relations advisor for private functions is most advantageous in the pre-construction/remodelling stage.

Why?

An experienced function planner understands what your customers will respond to: privacy and easy access, lack of obstructions in the room, audio-visual friendliness, separate bar facilities, and convenience to bathrooms.

This planner will also understand your needs: easy access to kitchen and storage areas without slowing service to other dining areas.

Developing business for these rooms begins even before you open your restaurant and requires special attention, for at least the first year, to build it to a healthy level.

You should expect your PR agent to help you create your restaurant's image, consulting on the logo to be used for your promotional efforts, and also on your interior and exterior signage and your menu design.

When it's finally time to open, VIP's, friends, and other potential customers can be invited to an opening night party. But the pre-opening publicity campaign should lead up to a press event for an "official opening" about two to three months after your actual opening. That gives your operation time to shake down.

Pre-opening publicity to the media should give them background information on the restaurant owners and what is being planned for this new restaurant.

After a program like this, the Morgan Williams restaurant in New York's financial center received considerable media attention about the opening month offer of a free bottle of wine (from a limited list) with dinner for two or more.

This was picked up by the "What's Happening" column of the *New York Daily News* and *The New York Times'* "Event Calendar," among others.

Many restaurants choose to support a charity as part of building an involvement with the community. Morgan Williams adopted the Westchester Chapter of Friends of Autistic Children and hosted a black-tie dinner. Even though it was on a Saturday night when the restaurant is normally closed because of its business district location, the dinner attracted 100 people paying $100 each, to net $6,000 for the charity.

Many items were donated for this event, including a top door prize of a trip for two to Bermuda.

The next two years saw the theme change to a Halloween costume party (on the Saturday closest to Halloween) with the charity netting $14,000 and then $21,000.

Harbour Lights, a 350-seat restaurant with a private room, a semi-private room, and an outside deck available for private functions, opened at the South Street Seaport in New York in November of 1987.

Press releases to night-life publications and entertainment columnists in the daily newspapers played up the restaurant's ambience and its beautiful view of the harbor.

A grand opening event was delayed until June, when the Seaport location was even more attactive. One hundred and fifty invitations were sent to consumer press, editors of trade and meetings publications, and meeting planners at major local businesses.

Forty-five key people (over 30 were meeting planners) showed up for hors d'oeuvres, cocktails, and press kits.

A follow-up thank you letter included an invitation to return with a companion as the restaurant's guests for dinner.

Within two months bookings were being made, and only two years after it opened, Harbour Lights booked about 500 private functions.

Of course, Harbour Lights didn't stop reaching out with that reception. After Labor Day, when the city was putting summer pleasures behind, a mailing to 400 local personnel directors invited them to call for an appointment to tour the facilities and have an Irish coffee "by the fire".

The aim was to develop Christmas party business; 25 personnel directors accepted this invitation.

Another restaurant in the South Street Seaport area is The Yankee Clipper, opened in 1984. To promote "the most extensive vintage port wine list in New York," they hosted a port tasting seminar—vintage vs. wood ports.

About 50 representatives of the consumer and trade press attended a 5 to 6 P.M. seminar followed by an hour spent tasting the port wines and enjoying selected hors d'oeuvres.

Each guest also received an invitation for two to return for a complimentary dinner.

In addition to the immediate publicity that this generated, six months later an editor called in search of information for a feature article on port wines. Yankee Clipper had become the "expert" on this subject.

Remember that public relations is much more than sending news releases to your local media.

HOW TO SPONSOR CHARITY EVENTS

Allow a one-year lead time. Choose a charity that has a special appeal to you or to your community, then meet with the director of that charity.

Assuming that your efforts are welcomed, together invite a local celebrity to serve as honorary chairperson of the event. You want permission to use the celebrity's name to lend prestige to the party and, of course, hope she or he will attend. Don't ask any more of your new chairperson, but if more is offered, accept it.

Next, take a shot at a corporate sponsor, understanding that generally the corporation will want to wait for the second year of the event.

What you want from a corporate sponsor:

1) A donation to the charity, commensurate with the expected public relations benefits to the sponsor.

2) Access to contacts who might participate by either attending the event, donating directly to the charity, or donating door prizes.

3) Key corporate people to show the flag by attending the event.

No further demands on the corporate sponsor's time should be made or expected.

Prepare a formal proposal for the potential sponsor, outlining the event, its purpose, who will be attending, the publicity plan, and the benefits to the corporation you are soliciting.

Draw up a list of targets by asking your regular customers who at their companies might be receptive. Use your own contacts—suppliers, friends, relatives—as well, of course.

Set up a meeting at your prospect's office and be businesslike. Submit the written proposal and request a follow-up meeting where the corporation can contribute its ideas to make the event even more successful.

It's important to have your PR person, who should have helped prepare the proposal, with you at this meeting. After you have greeted your prospect and briefly described the charity and your planned event, turn the meeting over to your PR Representative to make the pitch and ask for the order.

You remain the nice guy. If the prospect decides to say no, he can still feel comfortable visiting your restaurant and even attending the charity event.

Inform each corporation that you are contacting other firms also. The first commitment will get the sponsorship, along with an option on succeeding events.

52

THE COMPLEAT MANAGER

As a restaurant owner, one of your major jobs is to develop,strong managers who can execute your concepts and bring fresh thinking to your planning meetings.

Only with a good management team in place can you be free to concentrate on growing your business, improving your one location, or opening additional restaurants with the same or a different concept.

That advice comes from from Neil S. Reyer, vice president of restaurant and travel management for Chemical Bank, New York. He runs Chemical's corporate dining facilities, including special events and conferences. In the restaurant business since 1958, he is a keen observer of the scene and writes for *Nation's Restaurant News* and *Restaurant Hospitality* magazines among others.

"The nation's two-and four-year colleges are graduating a large pool of people well trained in culinary arts and restaurant management. These graduates offer good potential leaders," he said. "However, you have to work hard to develop that potential in your new employee before you can impose management responsibilities and expect them to be executed to your satisfaction."

Reyer believes strongly that today's restaurant manager must be familiar with all of the government regulations affecting restaurateurs, including the edicts of the alphabet soup that includes the FDA (Food and Drug Administration), USDA (U.S. Department of Agriculture), and OSHA (Occupational Safety and Health Act). A manager also must be capable of dealing with

172

horses that work hard for you in bringing patrons back and in generating positive word of mouth."

As a consultant, Anderson concerns himself primarily with: 1) The menu. A well-planned menu dictates whether a profit can be made or not 2) Management attitude towards customers, food, and service.3) Staff training.

His philosophies were put to the test in 1984 when Oklahoma entered a harsh economic recession and the family restaurant he owned and managed had a 48 percent decline in business over 18 months.

Until then, he admits, business had been good and he had been slack about overseeing the operation. In order to stay in business, that had to change. He applied his menu engineering principles to generate more profits and instituted almost weekly training meetings with a serious emphasis on food quality, cleanliness, and service.

A regular weekly advertising program in the local newspaper featured three specials, changing each week. He reprinted menus twice a year to highlight seasonal foods and to force him to focus on menu engineering at least those two times a year.

Sales have increased every year since then.

To keep himself and his students up to date, he recently inaugurated a program working with local business people. A restaurateur visits the classroom, hands out copies of the menu, and describes the restaurant's operation, the choices on the menu, and the food costs and sales figures for every menu item.

Students spend the next four weeks analyzing this data, which is kept confidential. They then produce a report and suggestions for redesigning the menu to make it a better sales tool.

Anderson reports that restaurateurs, impressed with the reports, have implemented many of the class suggestions.

This same type of in-the-trenches involvement with the restaurant business is taking place at restaurant schools in every part of the country.

If a consultant could benefit your restaurant, contact the Council of Hotel, Restaurant and Institutional Educators for the name of a college program close to you. The address and phone number is CHRIE, 1200 17th Street, N.W., 7th Floor, Washington, D.C. 20036. Telephone: (202) 331-5990.

54

THE HOST WITH THE MOST

"The idea that the restaurant business is show business is not new," said Larry Soll, president of Vernon Consulting, a restaurant consulting firm based in Scarsdale, New York. "I wasn't around at the time, no matter what people say, but the excitement of the Gay Nineties didn't come from TV dinners. It came from splashy nightclubs and elegant restaurants, like New York's world-famous Delmonico's.

"The most successful restaurateur that I have known was Sherman Billingsly, the Oklahoma-born proprietor of the Stork Club, the place to be seen during the 1930s and '40s.

"He personified the host who made dining a special enjoyment. The Stork Club attracted a sophisticated clientele and Billingsly nurtured the clubs's mystique by presenting favored women guests with a bottle of Stork Club perfume, prepared exclusively for him in a striking package.

"Men knew they were in the select group when they were given Stork Club suspenders, bright fire-engine red with a subtle Stork Club emblem.

"Of course, the business has changed since then, but it just means you have to work harder at basics like showmanship. The good news is that there is help for you, if you just ask for it.

"One example is the German Wine Information Bureau. It would like more Americans to know that German wines marry very well with food. They have collected authentic German food recipes and can tell you which wines go best with what recipe. At times, colorful posters and table tents are available."

The same type of cooperation is generally available from California's Wine Institute, Foods and Wines From France, Wines From Spain, The New York State Wine Council, the Cling Peach Advisory Board, and similar organizations.

These trade groups can frequently be contacted at local or national trade shows, or local suppliers might be able to help.

Soll suggests that you plan on a full year's calendar of special events that would commence in four to six months. Notify suppliers of your schedule and invite their suggestions on how their products can fit into your promotional themes and how they can provide merchandising help.

Tell them you'll accept suppliers' input up to 90 days before each themed event, which allows you enough time to promote a successful turnout.

"The help is there," said Soll. "Track it down and ask for it."

55

FLAIR AND ENOUGH CAPITAL BUILD SUCCESS

After 27 years of successfully owning and operating restaurants in New York City, Tom Slattery decided to embark on a career as a restaurant consultant.

"For years I had been giving away good advice on how to open and run a profitable restaurant," Slattery said, "and I finally decided it was time to make this a full time career."

But some habits are hard to break. He paused one more time to give away advice, sharing some of the lessons he's learned over the years, most recently as a partner in Rumm's, a restaurant on Manhattan's East Side.

For instance, on the subject of opening a new restaurant:

1) Decide the type of restaurant you want to run and then find an area that needs that kind of restaurant. Or, flip it around. Find the area that you want to be in and determine what type of restaurant that area needs.

2) Under-capitalization is the major reason that new restaurants fail. Get a qualified restaurant consultant, one who has dealt with at least two complete renovations and knows the workings of contractors and sub-contractors, to help estimate opening costs.

3) Don't try to save money by skirting building codes. It always winds up costing you more. Have enough money to cover 50 percent more than you project for opening costs plus the first six months of operation, assuming that business will be slow.

4) Create activity and excitement right from the beginning and don't stop. That will draw the customers in. Though it might be slow at first, if you're doing everything else right, the extra capital you've projected will keep you in business until there are enough patrons to show a profit.

5) Don't be afraid to take that extra step. When opening a restaurant, many people go 80 to 90 percent of the way and then stop, often because they run out of money. Don't stop. Buy the paintings, plants, and artifacts that will establish the special look of your restaurant. If necessary, postpone buying kitchen or other equipment you won't need right away.

6) Whatever you do, do it with a flair. Don't just pass out flyers for your promotions. Most of them will quickly fly into file 13. Roll them up and tie them with a ribbon or circle them with a colorful rubber band. Create a need for people to want to look at your message, so important that you've taken the trouble to gift-wrap it.

Understand also that people will judge your restaurant by the appearance of the people distributing your flyers.

7) Locks are meant to keep honest people honest. Don't tempt a good person too often.

Secure all storage areas with some sort of enclosure. Even chicken wire will deter spur-of-the-moment temptations. A three-foot-thick steel vault door won't stop the professional thief.

Total lack of supervision inevitably leads to mischief. Where continual supervision is not possible, creation of an omni-presence is ideal. One way to create the illusion that you are always there is to practice irregular arrivals. Don't be predictable as to when you'll walk through the door.

Slattery wears another hat, serving as president of the Manhattan Restaurant Association for the past 10 years.

"It's important for restaurateurs to band together—whether it's to fight beauracratic harassment, to get access to low-cost insurance and legal advice or to keep up with developments that can affect your success," he said.

What is success in the restaurant business?

"It's very difficult to make much more than a living," he warned. "The reality is that many owners or investors are just buying themselves a job, and not a very well-paying one, if you count it on an hourly basis.

"If you are thinking of yourself as a non-working investor, don't expect to make a big profit on your investment. In fact, if you just want to be part owner of a restaurant, don't invest in one that has to start from scratch. Find a good restaurant owned by people who know what they are doing but started without enough capital. Invest enough money with them so that they can blossom and you'll be helping to make a 'success' happen.

"But make sure your partners have a sense of humor and know enough to have fun while they work."

Part IV

SIGNATURE RECIPES

The Ballroom
New York, New York

CAZUELA DE CHORIZO
SPANISH SAUSAGE STEW WITH PAPRIKA AND TOMATO SAUCE

3 tbsps olive oil
1 medium onion, finely chopped
2 garlic cloves, finely chopped
½ tsp chopped fresh thyme or pinch of
dried ½ bay leaf
7 links of chorizo or other spicy sausage, thinly sliced
1 tsp paprika
1 tsp all purpose flour
¼ cup dry white wine
⅓ cup good quality tomato sauce
⅓ cup water
8 small boiling potatoes, boiled and peeled
¼ cup chopped parsley

1. Heat oil in large skillet over medium heat. Add onion, garlic, thyme and bay leaf and cook, stirring just until onion is translucent, about 5 minutes.

2. Add chorizo and saute until golden brown, about 4 minutes. Add paprika and flour and stir to coat chorizo. Cook 2 to 3 minutes, pour in wine and cook briefly until it evaporates.

3. Stir in tomato sauce and water. Lower heat and simmer gently, uncovered, until sauce just coats chorizo, about 5 minutes. Serve hot over boiled potatoes. Sprinkle with parsley.

6 to 8 servings.

CARACOLES CON FRIJOLES COLORADOS
SNAILS WITH RED BEANS

4 tbsps olive oil
2 tbsps (¼ stick) unsalted butter
⅓ cup finely chopped shallot
2 garlic cloves, finely chopped
2 small fresh chilies, split lengthwise, seeded and finely chopped
Pinch of freshly grated nutmeg
Pinch of ground cloves
Pinch of ground cumin
1 can snails (6 or 7½ oz.) drained, rinsed and patted dry
2 tbsps Pernod
1 cup beef stock or water
4 cups cooked red kidney beans (soak 1 ½ cups dried beans overnight in 4 cups of water, drain, place in pot with water to cover by 2 inches and bring to a boil. Simmer covered over medium heat until tender) or 2 one-pound cans drained and rinsed.
½ cup chopped parsley
Salt and freshly ground pepper

1. Heat 2 tbsps each of oil and butter in a large skillet over medium high heat. Add shallot aand garlic and saute, stirring constantly, until lightly golden, about 3 minutes. Add chilies, nutmeg, cloves and cumin and stir 2 minutes.

2. Add snails and cook, stirring occasionally, 5 minutes. Add Pernod and cook until it evaporates.

3. Add beef stock, bring to boil and cook, stirring 2 to 3 minutes. Add beans and ¼ cup parsley, stirring briefly just until beans are heated through. Remove from heat and stir in remaining 2 tbsps olive oil and salt and pepper to taste. Sprinkle with remaining ¼ cup parsley and serve warm.

6 to 8 servings.

PAPAS A LA AREQUIPUENA
POTATO BALLS WITH ROASTED CHILIES, WALNUTS AND CHEESE

3 dried ancho chilies (available in Latin America markets) split lengthwise and seeded
⅓ cup annato seed (Latin American markets)
1 cup vegetable oil
Potato Mixture
3 pounds of potatoes (about 8 medium), peeled, cooked and mashed
Juice of 1 lime or lemon

Sauce:
Coarse salt
1 cup olive oil
2 small fresh chilies, split lengthwise, seeded and coarsely chopped
1 garlic clove, peeled
1¼ cup walnuts (5 oz.)
2 tsps salt
½ pound Greek feta cheese, crumbled
Freshly ground pepper
Lettuce leaves
2 hard cooked eggs, peeled and sliced
1 ear of corn, shucked, boiled until tender and thinly sliced through cob
¼ cup cilantro (coriander) leaves, chopped
Calamata olives (garnish)

1. Hold each chili with fork over gas flame, turning until lightly roasted on all sides. Place in bowl with 2 cups warm water, soak 20 minutes.

2. Prepare achiote oil by stirring together annato seeds and vegetable oil in saucepan over medium heat 2 minutes, remove from heat and cool. Oil will keep indefinitely, tightly covered, in a cool place.

3. For potato mixture: Stir ¼ cup achiote oil into mashed potatoes. Add lime or lemon juice and salt to taste. Set aside.

4. For sauce: Drain ancho chilies, reserving soaking liquid, and place in processor with olive oil, fresh chilies and garlic. Process until smooth. With machine running, add ½ cup walnuts, ½ cup of the reserved soaking liquid and 2 tsps salt, process until smooth. Add half of crumbled cheese and process until smooth. Transfer to small bowl. Coarsely chop remaining walnuts, add to mixture with remaining cheese, salt and pepper to taste.

5. Shape potato mixture into about 2 dozen 1 ½ inch balls. Arrange on lettuce leaves, spooning a little sauce on top. Garnish with eggs, corn, coriander and olives. Serve at room temperature.

    6 to 8 servings.

Clary's American Grill
Springfield, Missouri

ANAHEIM CHILI SOUP

Saute in 1 pound of butter:
2 diced green peppers
2 diced red peppers
2 medium diced yellow onions
2 27oz. cans diced green chilies
4 cloves diced garlic
1 stalk diced celery

When vegetables are soft, add:
2 cups flour
4 tbsps cumin
1 tbsp chili powder
1 tsp cayenne

Cook until flour taste is gone and add:
3 quarts hot water
3 ripe, seeded chopped tomatoes
3 whole, boneless, skinless chicken breast cut into
½ inch cubes
½ pound chicken base

Stir constantly until it simmers and then add ½ gallon heavy
cream. Salt and pepper to taste.

GRAND MARNIER SOUFFLES

10oz. corn starch (by weight)
10oz. sugar (by weight)
$^5/_6$ tbsp salt
40oz. milk
5oz. butter

Mix all, stirring constantly over medium heat until very thick. (Thick pudding consistency).

20 eggs, separated
20 yokes: add ¾ cup liqueur plus 2 tbsps orange compound and mix.
20 whites: Whip until they form soft peaks, then gradually add $^5/_6$ tbsp cream of tartar and $^5/_6$ cup sugar, mix until stiff peaks are formed.

Let pudding mix cool slightly, add flavored yoke mix. Fold in meringue carefully until well incorporated.

Butter and sugar 20 6oz. souffle cups, add souffle mix carefully until almost full. Bake in 350 degree convection oven for 20 minutes or until done.

Serves 20

Eamonn Doran's
New York, New York

GAELTACH CHICKEN (GALE-TOCK)

One(1) 4 lbs. chicken
½ orange
½ onion
2 tbsp melted margarine, butter or oil

1. Put orange and onion in body of chicken and secure with skewer.
2. Place chicken in roasting pan and rub oil or butter over breast and legs.
3. Cover with foil and roast for not more than 1½ hours in a moderate oven, 350 degrees F.

SAVORY STUFFING

3 large slices crustless white bread
2 tbsps chopped parsley
1 tsp chopped thyme, ½ small onion
Liver of the chicken, chopped
½ cup milk
Pinch each of nutmeg, salt and pepper

1. Soak bread in milk (not too wet)
2. Add all other ingredients, mix thoroughly and season
3. Place in dish and bake in oven for approximately 1 hour at 350 degrees, along with the chicken.

LEMON SAUCE

1 tsp butter
1 tsp flour
1 cup ham stock (hot)
1 lemon

1. Melt butter, add flour and mix well.
2. Add ham stock, stir well until it boils.
3. Add grated lemon peel and juice of the lemon, stir again.

BOILED HAM (IN CIDER)

1 whole ham
2 quarts cider
Dried mustard, cloves, bread crumbs and brown sugar.

1. Steep ham overnight in cold water
2. Drain, then add cider, mustard and enough cold water to cover ham.
3. Bring slowly to a boil, allowing 20 to 25 minutes per pound.
4. Let ham sit for 1 hour in liquid, then take it from pot and remove skin.
5. Coat fat on ham with bread crumbs mixed with brown sugar and stud with cloves.
6. Brown in a hot oven for 5 to 10 minutes.

Serve chicken, garnished with ham, lemon sauce and savory stuffing.

BRAISED IRISH LAMB STEW

2 pounds neck and shoulder of lamb,
trim, debone and cut in strips
2 tbsp oil
2 large onions, diced
2 tomatoes, chopped
½ tsp paprika
1 clove garlic, crushed
¼ pint stock
salt and pepper
Optional: 1 medium green or red pepper

1. Heat oil in heavy pan.
2. Brown lamb on both sides, leaving it rare.
3. Transfer lamb to casserole dish.
4. Add onions, tomatoes and garlic to pan, sprinkle with paprika and fold.
5. Add stock, salt and pepper, stirring well and bring to boil for about 2 seconds.
6. Pour over lamb in casserole dish and place in 350 degree oven for approximately 1½ hours.
7. Serve with boiled potatoes and string beans flavored with smoked bacon strips, garnish with parsley.

Elizabeth On 37th
Savannah, Georgia

COUNTRY SHRIMP WITH SAFFRON RICE

¼ cup country ham or Prosciutto, minced
¼ cup minced shallots
½ cup minced leek
¼ cup minced green onion
2 tbsps minced elephant garlic (this is very mild garlic, if regular garlic is used, only use 1 tsp)
2 tbsps olive oil
2 tbsp peanut oil
1½ pounds large shrimp, peeled, deveined, tails left on
2 tbsp cornstarch mixed with ¼ tsp white pepper (no salt needed as country ham is salty)
½ cup cream
2 tomatoes, peeled, seeded and finely diced
1 tsp Minor shrimp base, if available

Place the two oils, country ham, shallots, leeks, green onion and garlic in a large saute pan with a lid. Cover and saute for five minutes. Dust the shrimp with the cornstarch/white pepper mix and add to the pan. Cover and saute until shrimp are lightly pink, shaking the pan occasionally.

Add the cream, tomato and shrimp base. Do not cover. Shake the pan lightly as the cream reduces to form a lovely tomato cream sauce. Serve with steamed asparagus and saffron rice.

SAFFRON RICE

¼ cup minced onions
2 tbsp butter
1 large pinch of saffron
3½ cups of chicken broth
1½ cups white rice
Salt and pepper to taste

Saute the onion and butter briefly. Add the saffron, salt, pepper, rice and chicken broth. Bring to a boil. Reduce the heat, cover

and simmer for about 20 minutes until the rice absorbs the
broth.
Serves 4

PECAN CREAM PIE

Pre-bake 3 pie shells (pate brisee)

Filling:
1½ cups firm packed brown sugar
2 tbsps unflavored gelatin
2 cups sour cream
6 tbsps unsalted butter, melted
8 extra large eggs, separated
2 tsps vanilla
2 cups toasted chopped pecans

Topping:
1 quart whipping cream, whipped with:
2 tbsps good bourbon
⅓ cup sugar
1 cup toasted chopped pecans

In a large sauce pan combine the brown sugar, gelatin, sour
cream, butter and egg yolks. Whisk over medium flame until
the mixture thickens and steam rises. Continue whisking off
the flame until the mixture cools a bit. Add vanilla and refrigerate until mixture begins to set about 45 minutes.

Fold in 2 cups toasted chopped pecans.

Beat the egg whites (which have been left at room temperature)
until firm. Whisk ¼ of the beaten whites into the pecan cream
and then fold the remaining egg whites into the lightened
mixture. Spoon into the three shells. This mixture should fill
each shell to about one half full.

Chill.

Top with a thick layer of the firmly whipped bourbon-cream.
Sprinkle with the remaining cup of toasted pecans.

Giannotti Steak House
Norridge, Illinois

VESUVIO POTATOES

Quarter Idaho potatoes, with skin, lengthwise. Deep fry for 10
minutes, remove from the fryer and put into skillet, adding
salt, pepper, garlic, oregano and white wine. Place in oven,
uncovered, for 10 minutes.

8 FINGER CAVATELLI

A local lady makes strips of cavatelli from scratch, then rolls them
with her 8 fingers to thin the dough out. Then cover with a
marinara sauce, add butter, Parmesan cheese and a very little
bit of cayenne pepper.

Goodale's Restaurant
Closed years ago when Percy Goodale retired

GOODALE'S LOBSTER STEW

6 oz. milk
½ tsp Worcestershire sauce
2 tsp butter
4 oz. lobster meat
chopped parsley

Warm the lobster meat in milk and butter. Add worcestershire
sauce, heat but do not boil, traansfer to a hot bowl, add parsley
sparingly and, after placing in front of customer, add a dash of
sherry.

Tony May
2 Selected recipes from his book, Italian Cuisine, Basic Cooking Techniques

VEAL CHOP VALDOSTANA

4 veal chops
4 oz. Fontina cheese
salt and pepper
white truffle (optional)
1 egg, beaten
white bread crumbs
3 oz. butter

Butterfly the veal chops, leaving them attached to the bone. Flatten slightly and place slices of Fontina cheese in between the two pieces of meat, salt and pepper to taste and pound the edges together with a mallet. Then dip in the beaten egg and the bread crumbs. Melt the butter in a skillet. When hot, place the veal chops in and cook for 2 minutes on each side, then 3 more minutes in the oven at 450° F. Remove to serving platter and add a shaving of white truffles.

(See next Page for the other recipe)

VITELLO TONNATO
VEAL IN TUNA SAUCE

2 pounds butt tenderloin
3 cups white wine
1 celery stalk
1 carrot
1 small onion
2 cloves
7 oz. tuna in oil
6 anchovy fillets
2 hard boiled egg yolks
2 lemons: 1 squeezed, 1 thinly sliced
½ cup oil
2 tbsps capers
1 tbsp white vinegar

Let the meat marinate in the wine, celery, carrot, chopped onion and cloves for one day. Remove the meat from the marinade, wrap and tie tightly in a cheesecloth and place in an oval pan just large enough to hold it together. Put back in the marinade and cook slowly for about one hour. Remove from heat and let the meat cool in its cooking liquid.

De-grease and filter the cooking liquid. Blend the liquid in a food mill with the tuna, anchovies, 1 tbsp capers and egg yolks. Dilute the sauce with lemon juice and vinegar and whisk in the oil in a steady stream until a velvety sauce is achieved (similar to mayonnaise). Slice the veal and, after spreading a few tbsp of sauce on a serving platter, add the veal one layer at a time, with sauce covering each layer. Sprinkle with Capers. Garnish with lemon slices.

McCully's Rooftop Restaurant
Bonita Springs, Florida

ROAST PORK LOIN CALYPSO

2 center cut pork loins, bone in
1 quart chicken stock
1 pound brown sugar
¼ cup dark rum
4 tsp minced garlic
4 tsp ground ginger
1 tsp ground clove
2 tsp salt
½ tsp pepper
½ cup light rum
Arrowroot and water to thicken
6 tbsps fresh lime juice

Preheat oven to 350 degrees. Place pork loins on rack in roasting pan and roast for 1 hour or until browned. In a stainless steel bowl, mix dark rum, ginger, cloves, garlic and brown sugar. Season lightly with salt and pepper. Remove roasts from the oven and degrease roasting pans.

Add the chicken stock to roasting pan. Spread the brown sugar/ rum glaze equally over the pork roasts and return to oven for another 30 minutes or till roasts reach 150 degrees. Do not overcook. In a saute pan, ignite the light rum and allow flame to die down. Add to stock in roasting pan, bring to a boil and thicken with arrowroot.

Finish the sauce with fresh lime juice and remove from heat. It is important to taste the sauce and adjust the seasonings and sweetness of the sauce. Slice the pork loins in one inch thick chops, topped with 2 ounces of sauce and a lime slice.

Serves 20

GROUPER MAISON

10 6oz. Grouper fillets
8 bananas, quartered
10oz. light brown sugar
bread crumbs for sprinkling
7½ cups pineapple juice
2½ cups bearnaise sauce
10oz. sliced almonds, toasted

Serves 10

1. Lay grouper out on a baking pan and place 3 quarters of bananas on top of each fillet.
2. Top with brown sugar and breadcrumbs, then pour pineapple juice onto baking pan.
3. Bake in the oven until grouper is firm to the touch, then plate it and finish with bernaise sauce and toasted almonds.

Pea Soup Andersen's
Buellton, California

ORIGINAL SPLIT PEA SOUP RECIPE

2 quarts of soft water
2 cups of Andersen's specially selected green split peas
1 branch of celery, coarsely chopped
1 large carrot, chopped
1 small onion, chopped
¼ tsp ground thyme
1 Bayleaf salt pepper

Boil all ingredients hard for 20 minutes, then slowly until peas are tender. Strain through a fine sieve and reheat to boiling point.

Philander's
Oak Park, Illinois

BARBECUE SHRIMP

12 shrimp
½ tsp pepper
1 tsp olive oil
½ pound melted butter
¼ tsp paprika

Preheat oven to 450 degrees. Mix all ingredients in ovenproof casserole dish and bake for 10 to 15 minutes.

One to two servings.

Linguini with Spicy Lobster

1 pound lobster, cooked
1 oz. olive oil
1 clove garlic, chopped
½ tsp crushed red pepper
1 cup chardonnay wine
1 quart heavy cream
Salt and pepper
1 Italian plum tomato, seeded and chopped
½ pound linguini, cooked and drained

Saute garlic and pepper in olive oil for 1 to 2 minutes. Add wine, cooking over medium heat reduce to ¼ cup. Add cream, cook over low heat for 15 to 20 minutes. Salt and pepper to taste. Remove meat from cooked lobster and add to sauce with chopped and seeded tomato. Heat thoroughly and serve on linguini.

Serves two to three.

FLOUNDER WITH TARRAGON

1 tsp beef paste
¼ cup water
½ pound butter, cut into small pieces
1 tsp fresh tarragon minced or ½ tsp dried
Pinch of black pepper
1 pound flounder
Melted butter
Dry bread crumbs
Dry vermouth

Combine beef paste, water and butter in double boiler set over boiling water. Whisk until butter is melted, then add tarragon and pepper. Brush flounder with this mixture and coat one side of fish with bread crumbs, placing on baking sheet, crumb side up. Sprinkle with splash of dry vermouth and broil for 5 to 8 minutes. Serve with tarragon sauce.

The Sardine Factory
Monterey, California

MONTEREY BAY PRAWN "CALIFORNIA"

24 extra large prawns, peeled and deveined
4 tsps minced fresh garlic
4 tsps minced fresh shallots
8 tbsps sliced fresh mushrooms
4 tbsps chopped fresh tomatoes
4 oz. Tequila
2 oz. Triplesec
2 oz. lime juice
4 tsps minced fresh chives
4 tbsps raw unsalted butter
salt and black pepper to taste
3 oz. olive oil

1. Add olive oil to hot saute pan
2. Carefully add prawns to oil and cook briefly
3. Add mushrooms, tomatoes, garlic, shallots, chives, salt and pepper and toss all ingredients in saute pan
4. Pull saute pan away from fire and add Tequila and Triplesec. Return pan to fire and flame pan. Add lime juice.
5. Remove prawns from saute pan and place on serving dish.
6. Return pan to fire, add butter and reduce liquid to create the sauce.
7. Pour sauce over prawns and serve immediately.

Suggested wine to be served with this dish:
La Reina Chardonnay 1987

Serves 6

PUMPKIN CHEESECAKE

Crumb Crust:
1½ cups graham cracker crumbs
6 tbsp butter, melted
¼ cup granulated sugar

Cream Cheese Filling:
2½ pounds cream cheese
1 cup sugar
4 whole eggs, lightly beaten
3 egg yolks, lightly beaten
3 tbsp all purpose flour
2 tsp ground cinnamon
1 tsp ground ginger
1 tsp ground cloves
1 cup heavy cream
1 tbsp vanilla extract
1 pound mashed pumpkin

1. Preheat oven to 425 degrees F.
2. In a large mixing bowl, beat together cream cheese, sugar, eggs and egg yolks.
3. Add flour and spices.
4. Beat in the heavy cream and vanilla extract, then add the mashed pumpkin and beat at medium speed on electric mixer until just mixed thoroughly.
5. Pour the mixture into the prepared crust and bake for 15 minutes. Reduce oven temperature to 275 degrees and bake for an additional hour. Turn off the oven but leave the cake in the oven overnight to cool.
6. Serve either warm or chilled with whipped cream.

FROZEN LEMON ZEST SOUFFLE

1 cup egg whites
1 cup plus 2 tbsps sugar
¾ cup creme patissiere*
grated peel of 4 lemons
juice of 4 lemons
1½ pints heavy cream (whipped unsweetened)

Warm egg whites and sugar in bowl over hot water. Remove from heat and beat with rotary beater until stiff. Mix creme patissiere with lemon peel and juice, fold in egg whites, fold in whipped cream, pour into souffle dish. Freeze at least 6 hours.

*CREME DE PATISSIERE (PASTRY CREAM)

1 quart milk
8 egg yolks
1 cup plus 2 tbsp sugar
¾ cup flour
½ tsp vanilla extract

Scald the milk. Beat egg yolks with sugar until mixture is pale yellow. Beat in flour, gradually pour in hot milk, beating all the time. Pour into sauce pan and cook, beating with wire whisk until smooth and thick. Remove from heat and stir in vanilla extract. Makes 3 cups.

Serves 6

RASPBERRY COOLER
(USING FROZEN LEMON ZEST SOUFFLE RECIPE).

Raspberries:
1 pound fresh or frozen raspberries (thawed).
1 cup granulated sugar. Makes two cups.

Put raspberries and sugar in electric blender at medium speed
for 2 minutes, strain to take out pits, refrigerate for 2 hours.

Vanilla Sauce:
1 cup milk
4 egg yolks
3 oz. sugar
½ tsp vanilla

Boil milk, mix yolks, sugar and vanilla. When milk is boiling, pour
yolk mixture into milk. Take off flame just before boiling, pour
into a bowl, place bowl over ice to cool.

Presentation:

Option 1: Vanilla Sauce put on plate first. Frozen Lemon Zest
Souffle "round" centered on top of sauce. Raspberry mix
poured diagonally across Sauce and Souffle.

Option 2: Same as above but Raspberry mix is put down, with a
swirl effect, on the sauce surrounding the souffle.

Signature Drinks Build Business

"I always promote signature drinks that my customers can only get when they visit my bar," says veteran bartender Jim Bradfield. "Not only do they come in more often, but they bring friends in to try Jimmy's latest new drink, and that friend keeps coming back, too."

Bradfield tended bar at Sherman Billingsly's original Stork Club, in New York City, from 1957 through 1964, followed by stints at El Morocco, The Jaeger House, Charlie Brown's, The Ad Lib and Eamonn Doran's.

Of all of the signature drinks he has invented, his favorite is:

NEPTUNE'S FIRE:

    1½ oz. Tequila
    2 dashes Worcestershire sauce
    1 dash Tabasco
    2 dashes celery salt
    salt and pepper
    2 dashes Rose's lime juice
    6 oz. Clamato Juice
    1 tsp Horseradish

Shake well, serve over rocks and garnish with one medium size shrimp.

KATHLEEN GEYER STEADMAN

September 24, 1932 - August 31, 1990

Kathy and I celebrated our 34th wedding anniversary on August 4, 1990, over an elegant, candlelit dinner in the nurses' meeting room on her floor at Memorial Sloan Kettering Hospital in New York City.

We spoke of the future. She was going to win her battle with breast cancer, we both believed that. She had important work to complete, helping women who were trying to escape from addictions.

Kathy was a certified moderator for Women For Sobriety, an international self-help group. Through informal meetings, Women for Sobriety helps women overcome addiction problems by replacing self-defeating and negative attitudes with feelings of confidence, power and self-worth.

For over 30 years as a music educator, Kathy taught children that if they could talk they could sing. These same communication skills allowed her to be uniquely effective in giving hope to women who had lost hope.

Unfortunately, Kathy was not allowed to continue her work. In her memory, I am donating to Women For Sobriety one dollar for every copy of this book that is sold.

Women For Sobriety was founded by Jean Kirkpatrick, Ph.D. (not the U.N. ambassador). One of her statements of purpose is "Women For Sobriety is unique in that it is an organization of women for women. It recognizes woman's emerging role and her necessity for self esteem and self discovery to meet today's conflicts."

If you would like to adopt W.F.S. as a philanthropy, write to Women for Sobriety at P.O. Box 618, Quakertown, PA 18951. Telephone: (215) 536-8026.

RESTAURANT TRADE MAGAZINES

Canadian Hotel and Restaurant
777 Bay Street
Toronto MSW 1A7
Ontario, Canada

Cheers
352 Park Avenue South
New York, N.Y. 10010

Food Arts
387 Park Avenue South
8th Floor
New York, N.Y. 10016

Foodservice Hospitality
980 Yonge St.
Suite 400
Toronto, Ontario M4W 2J8
Canada

Foodservice Product News
104 Fifth Avenue
New York, N.Y. 10011-6901

Nation's Restaurant News
425 Park Avenue
New York, N.Y. 10022

Restaurant Business
633 Third Avenue
New York, N.Y. 10017

Restaurant Hospitality
1100 Superior Avenue
Cleveland, Ohio 44114

Restaurants & Institutions
1350 E. Tuohy
Des Plaines, IL 60018

Top Shelf
199 Ethan Allen Highway
Ridgefield, CT 06877

ALPHABETICAL INDEX TO RESTAURANTS AND SERVICES

ALPHABETICAL INDEX TO PEOPLE